Cheap
Easy

Rc   ritain's foremost vegetarian cookery writer and her books have won her popular
acc   parts of the English-speaking world.

              en in the vanguard of the revolution in our eating habits in recent years, as more
as r   ie consume less meat and take greater interest in healthy eating. She frequently
cont   o national magazines, gives cookery demonstrations and broadcasts on radio and
telev   se is also a professional astrologer and, with her husband, runs a computer-based
astro   service which provides personality profiles, forecasts and compatibility charts.
(For mc   et ils, please send SAE to Rose Elliot, PO Box 16, Eastleigh SO5 6BH, UK.)

Other Thorsons books by Rose Elliot

Vegan Feasts
The Bean Book
Low Fat, Low Sugar

Cheap
& Easy

**Fast, flavoursome and inexpensive
dishes from Britain's best-known writer
on vegetarian cookery**

ROSE ELLIOT

Thorsons

Thorsons
An Imprint of HarperCollins`
77-85 Fulham Palace Road,
Hammersmith, London W6 8JB

First published by Fontana 1988
Published by Thorsons 1995
This edition published by Thorsons 2000

10 9 8 7 6 5 4 3 2 1

Text illustrations by Helen Holroyd

A catalogue record for this book
is available from the British Library

ISBN 07225 3948 /

Printed and bound in Great Britain by
Woolnough Bookbinding Ltd, Irthlingborough, Northamptonshire

contents

To my daughters,
Kate, Meg and Claire
with all my love

introduction

CHEAP FOOD, GOOD FOOD

There's something very satisfying about producing a tasty, nourishing meal at a rock-bottom price – and not having to spend hours in the kitchen in order to do it.

Cheap food can undoubtedly be good food, tasty, healthy and quick to make.

There are in the world a wealth of colourful and delicious dishes which have sustained our forebears for generations and still do so today. These use basic, cheap foods which do not need elaborate refining or packaging. They are additive-free, full of fibre and packed with nutrients – and they taste great.

Along with these basic international recipes are favourites from an exciting and rapidly developing culinary art, vegetarian cookery. These, too, use the basic, unprocessed foods and bring further variety and interest to money-saving meals.

Including some of these dishes in your weekly menus can save you money; basing your week's menus entirely on them can cut your expenses by at least a third.

FEELING GOOD, LOOKING GREAT

Contrary to what people think, cheap meals can actually be better for you in terms of health and nutrition than richer, more expensive, meals. It's well known that during the last war, people in Britain were healthier on the meagre diet which rationing enforced. This is because such a diet relies on basic foods such as potatoes, pasta, wholewheat or wholemeal bread, grains and pulses (legumes). All these contain fibre, are rich in nutrients and free from additives. If you base your meals on these staples, include small quantities of eggs and dairy produce, have a good source of vitamin C each day and, if possible, a good serving of green vegetables, you will be well-nourished, look fit and feel good. Good sources of vitamin C are kiwi fruit, oranges or grapefruit, or some orange or grapefruit juice, a good salad, or a good serving of potatoes, a large piece of melon or a bowl of strawberries.

If you're overweight, you'll probably find that you shed the extra weight naturally, as long as you keep away from the desserts and puddings, pies and cakes, which provide extra fillers for families and very active people. Replace ordinary milk with skimmed (non-fat) milk and use reduced-fat cheese for useful savings in calories.

It's possible to save a great deal of time and money by following a few simple guidelines.

Use food in season

Buying fresh food in season makes good economic sense as well as ensuring that you get the best quality. If you grow your own produce and can freeze some of it, that saves even more money. Making use of some of the free wild food to be found, such as chestnuts, blackberries, bilberries and sea spinach – and mushrooms with expert identification – can be an extra occasional bonus, though probably not enough to make much difference to the weekly budget.

When you grow your own food – or pick wild produce – you know exactly where it's come from and you can avoid chemical fertilizers, pesticides and other chemicals. If growing or picking your own is out of the question, you might consider joining one of the increasingly popular box schemes which provide organically grown fruit and vegetables in season. Organic produce is nearly always a bit more expensive than non-organic, but I do think it's money well spent if your budget allows.

Buying organic also ensures that the food is pure and natural and free from GMOs. Even if you can't afford to go all the way with organic food, the Soil Association advises that we should try to buy organic carrots, lettuces, strawberries, bananas, milk, chocolate and soya products, because these are the ones treated with the most chemicals or, in the case of soya, most likely to contain GMOs. Unfortunately there are soya products in 60 percent of supermarket goods, so in order to avoid GMOs it's best to buy from one of the supermarkets which has guaranteed their produce to be free from them, if you can't buy organic. When buying organic, look for the Soil Association logo to be really sure of the quality.

Make full use of vegetables

Vegetables represent excellent value for money: they're full of nourishment, and, being high in fibre, they're filling and health-giving. Make them the basis of meals often – there are plenty of main-meal vegetable recipes in this book. Always try to serve a vegetable or salad alongside a main course, for extra interest and to make the more expensive ingredients go further.

Use the basic proteins

These are the grains, lentils, beans and pasta which have sustained generations the world over. Again, these are excellent value, both in terms of health and money. Add just small quantities of more concentrated proteins such as eggs, cheese and nuts to turn them into tasty and highly nutritious meals.

Plan ahead

This does not necessarily mean you have to plan out meals for a whole week, but it helps to think in terms of two or three days at a time, because it doesn't take any time to cook an extra amount of rice or lentils, and very little time to fry an extra onion, prepare a double quantity of potatoes, breadcrumbs or grated cheese or make some extra mashed potatoes, and these can really save time and effort in the future.

Here are some example of menus which 'think ahead'; you don't have to serve the second meal on the following day as leftovers will keep for at least a day, if not two or three, covered and refrigerated.

Lentil roast or *carrot and hazelnut roast* – make enough to serve once hot with roast potatoes, gravy and a cooked vegetable, and once cold in slices, with chutney or a yogurt and chopped herb dressing and some salad or hot boiled brown rice – and make extra of that while you're about it too – see below. When you're par-boiling the potatoes to roast them, do a double quantity and save some to make into a *potato hotpot* or *potato and mushroom gratin* – and while you're making the sauce for these, make a double quantity so you can quickly rustle up *easy mushrooms baked in cheese sauce* to serve with crusty bread another day.

If you're serving delicious *ratatouille* with some brown rice, do extra rice and make the second batch into a rice salad, for serving with crusty rolls and watercress another day. *Provençal gratin* – again, cook a double batch of brown rice, and use the second batch for *rice croquettes*.

When you're making mashed potatoes to serve with a meal, make a double quantity ready for topping a *cottage pie* or *red kidney bean and tomato pie*, or for making into *nutty potato cakes* as a quick meal to serve with a *green salad*, or perhaps a *Greek salad*, for added interest.

If you're making pastry, perhaps for a *cheese and onion pie* or *potato and mushroom pasties*, which make a good lunchbox item, prepare extra and make a quiche case, then you can quickly whizz up a *mixed vegetable quiche* or a *sweetcorn soufflé quiche* another day. If you make a bit extra on top of that, you can bake some *jam tarts*, which are a healthy treat for children when made with wholewheat pastry and a reduced sugar jam.

A basic semolina mix, can be used to make *cheese fritters* and *Italian gnocchi*, both of which are perennial favourites. The cheese fritters are good served with parsley sauce, chips or new potatoes and a freshly cooked vegetable; the gnocchi are nice with a tomato and onion salad.

Some recipes which you like and never get tired of are worth making in a double amount, so that you can have two servings of them in the week. *Cheese fritters* come into that category in my family, and I also very much like the hearty soup, *pistou*, with its Provençal flavouring. *Ratatouille*, which I've already mentioned, is a dish which I, personally, never get tired of. Make a double batch of this and you can serve it once hot with brown rice, then you can have the rest cold, as a salad, on another day, or you can use it to fill a baked quiche case or crêpes. You can also put the ratatouille in a shallow ovenproof dish, make some hollows in it and break an egg into each hollow, then bake in a moderate oven until the eggs are just set, and serve with crusty bread.

It's always useful to make more breadcrumbs than you need, especially if you've got a food processor to make them in and a freezer in which to store them. I keep breadcrumbs in a plastic bag in the freezer, ready for instant use, and whizz up leftover slices of bread and the ends of loaves to add to them. Then they're ready for dishes such as *stuffed cabbage rolls, tomato bread pudding* or *mushroom and tomato layer*.

Some dishes such as *stuffed baked potatoes, toad-in-the-hole, pasta with leeks and cheese, quick pizza, steamed vegetable pudding, macaroni cheese* or *macaroni bake*, are useful 'one-off' dishes, though you could cook enough macaroni for both the macaroni cheese and the bake while you're about it. If you also make extra cheese sauce when you're making the macaroni cheese, you'd be able to make *cauliflower, Stilton and walnut bake* very quickly the next day.

In fact, half an hour spent with this recipe book and a notepad and pencil working out some inter-related meals like this, which appeal to you, and making a shopping list, could save you several hours of time during the week.

One more time-saver and flavour-enhancer: I've found chopped fresh parsley to be invaluable in adding flavour to dishes made from cheap ingredients. It really is worth the expense – or, better still, worth the effort of growing some – lots in fact. Then wash and chop it by the handful so that you have a plastic bag of it in the freezer, ready for instant use.

KEEP THE BASICS

If you always keep a few staples in the storecupboard and fridge you'll be able to rustle up a quick meal in next to no time. For instance, with the following staples to hand, you could make any of the dishes suggested below them.

wholewheat flour	potatoes
Brazil nuts	carrots
green lentils	onions
split red lentils	garlic
wholewheat bread	lemons
canned tomatoes	

pasta	butter
rolled oats	eggs
dried thyme	cheese
dried basil or oregano	milk
olive oil	plain yogurt

Savoury Brazil nut fritters with a yogurt and chopped onion sauce or chutney; *golden lentil soup* with warm wholewheat bread; *potato and onion soup* with toasted cheese sandwiches; quick *French onion soup*; pasta with grated cheese; *potato and onion fry; even easier potato cakes; macaroni cheese, lentil roast* and, if you've got some mustard – or leave it out – *savoury bread and butter pudding*. And if you add to these basics a couple of courgettes (zucchini), a couple of sweet green peppers, some celery and some curry powder, you could also make *Spanish omelette, green lentil soup*, and *lentils with tomatoes and thyme*, for serving with crusty bread. And with some fresh ginger and parsley in your fridge and a bottle of chilli powder on the shelf, you could add to this list *spicy lentil burgers* and probably quite a few other quick and easy recipes in this book, too.

GIVE YOURSELF SOME TREATS

Lentil roast and cabbage, or pasta and grated cheese, may be great, healthy, money-saving food, but you need something a bit more luxurious every so often to keep your inspiration up. So plan for some special dishes sometimes. These may be a little more expensive or a little more trouble to make, but they're a nice change and a pleasant tonic. Dishes such as *cheese fondue* served with lots of crusty French bread and some dry white wine; *deep-fried Camembert* with some brown rice and apricot or mango chutney; a real *yeast pizza* which is fun to make and very satisfying, or *couscous with spicy chick pea stew*, delicious and fragrantly flavoured. Other dishes which are a bit special are *stuffed avocado*, which is nice served on a base of creamy, light mashed potato with a crunchy side salad; *aubergines provençales*, which are good with sauté or new potatoes and a cooked vegetable such as French (fine green) beans; *individual cheese soufflés* served with salad with a really good dressing; *la parmigiana* or **Middle Eastern chick pea stew**, both of which are good with crusty bread and some red wine; *spinach roulade with mushroom filling* with some lightly cooked carrots and French (fine green) beans or courgettes (zucchini); *cauliflower and green pea terrine* with crusty bread, tomato and onion salad and some wine; and *creamy pasta* with a green salad. *Mushroom-stuffed crêpes* can also be delicious, as can *vegetable rice with roasted nuts*, especially if you buy some whole roasted cashew nuts; and *carrot and ginger soup*, especially if you include the optional cream, or *Greek salad* as first courses.

Alternatively, if you have a sweet tooth, you may feel more like turning to the desserts and baking sections of this book for *sponge pudding, fruit crumble, quick and easy fruit cake, gingerbread* or *all-in-one sponge cake* as special treats.

POTS AND PANS

To make all these dishes, having the right equipment can save hours of time, as well as energy. However, cheap and easy cooking does not demand lots of complicated gadgets.

A food processor and an electric mixer do save time and effort, but they are only essential for a few of the recipes in this book. The rest rely on the minimum of simple equipment as follows:

A good sharp knife The traditional Sabatier ones are expensive but last well and once you've used one, you won't want to use anything else. Choose a steel or stainless steel one with a 13cm/5 inch blade and make sure it is the real thing, with the blade riveted into the handle. You'll need a steel to sharpen it on too.

A sturdy wooden chopping board A good size is 2.5cm/1 inch thick and not less than 40 x 30cm/16 x 12 inches. This will double as a board for rolling out pastry.

Clear glass bowls in several sizes

Several casserole dishes

A colander Preferably a stainless steel one, which will last for ever and can double as a steamer.

An egg whisk A metal balloon type is quite cheap to buy.

A frying pan Ideally it's useful to have two, one measuring 27.5cm/10¾ inches across, for general frying, and one measuring 20cm/8 inches across, for crêpes.

A rolling pin A plain wooden one without handles is best.

A box grater which you can stand on your chopping board and which has different sizes of holes.

A measuring jug

A set of measuring spoons

A palette knife (metal spatula)

A fish slice (slotted spatula)

Several wooden spoons of different sizes

A potato peeler

A large metal sieve (strainer) and a large nylon sieve (strainer)

A large, medium and small saucepan My preference is for stainless steel or good-quality enamel.

A pressure cooker Not essential, but useful for preparing beans and lentils quickly and for making soups. If you're buying a new one, choose a stainless steel one.

Kitchen scales are useful, but the recipes in this book have been planned so that these are not essential.

In addition to these basics, you'll need some old tablespoons, forks and teaspoons for cooking jobs; also various baking pans, a baking sheet or tray and a wire cooling rack.

Basic Staples: Dried and canned beans, canned tomatoes, lentils, pasta, wholewheat flours, rice and other grains. Buy in fairly small quantities from a store with a rapid turnover to ensure freshness. The same applies to nuts.

Dairy Produce: Free-range eggs, milk, yogurt, small amounts of cream and soured cream for occasional use. A basic Cheddar-type cheese for cooking – I use a vegetarian Cheddar – and the occasional use of other cheeses such as mozzarella, Camembert, Parmesan and soft white cheeses to add interest to meals.

Fats: Worth spending money on from the health point of view. My preference is for a good-quality unsalted butter on the table and for baking; virgin olive oil for salad dressings and dishes where the flavour is important, and groundnut (peanut) or olive oil for frying, because these oils are more stable at high temperatures and so healthier. Watch and cut back on the amount of fat you use, both to save money and make your food healthier.

Sweetenings: Choose real unrefined sugars where possible: dark molasses sugar for dishes which can take the flavour; lighter brown sugars or demerara sugar for more delicate flavours. A jar of vanilla sugar is useful to have for occasional use in delicate dishes – to make this, break a vanilla pod (bean) in half and bury the halves in a jar of caster (superfine) sugar. Clear honey, golden syrup (or light corn syrup) and black treacle (molasses) are handy for occasional use, as is jam: homemade or one of the reduced sugar or no-added-sugar jams.

Flavourings: Sea salt and black pepper which you will mill yourself in a grinder make all the difference to the flavour of dishes. Mustard powder is another useful flavouring, as are soy sauce – choose a natural one, without preservatives and colouring – yeast extract, lemon juice and Tabasco. Parsley is very useful, as I've already mentioned. Good vegetarian stock powders are useful for soups. Fresh basil is another extremely useful flavouring, as is fresh mint. Other useful herbs and spices, worth collecting gradually, are cardamom, cinnamon – ground and sticks – ginger, bay leaves, chilli powder, cloves, ground coriander, ground and whole cumin seeds, caraway seeds, dillweed, fennel seeds, turmeric, rosemary, thyme, mace, basil, oregano, mixed herbs, curry powder, paprika, ground ginger. Garlic salt and celery salt are useful for quick use. Fresh garlic and fresh ginger are also very useful flavourings. Vanilla pods (beans) and real vanilla extract are useful, so is nutmeg – buy it whole and grate on the fine edge of a box grater or with a special little nutmeg grater.

Wine vinegar is essential for making good salad dressings – I like the red wine vinegar best – and it's useful to have a jar of good-quality mayonnaise in the fridge.

super soups

Soups are wonderful time and money savers. They can be made extremely quickly and cheaply, and if you serve a soup at the beginning of the meal, not only is it warming and welcoming, it also means that the main course can be that much lighter. If you choose one of the 'big soups', such as pistou, lentil or leek and potato, it can be a main course in itself, so you don't have to bother with separate vegetables or any accompaniments, except perhaps for some warm bread rolls or, if you feel like preparing them, some dumplings or hot garlic or herb bread – see overleaf.

TO MAKE DUMPLINGS

Put 175g/6oz/1 cup + 3tbsp wholewheat flour into a bowl with 1½tsp baking powder, ½tsp salt and 65g/2½oz/5tbsp grated hard butter; mix together. Then add 1tsp yeast extract dissolved in 2tbsp water and mix; add more water, to make a soft dough. Then form into 8 even-sized balls. Drop the dumplings into a pan half full of gently simmering water and simmer them for 20 minutes, until puffed up. Drain them and serve with soup.

TO MAKE GARLIC OR HERB BREAD

Set the oven to 200°C/400°F/Gas 6. Blend a crushed garlic clove or 2tsp chopped fresh herbs, such as chives, thyme and marjoram, or the frozen chopped mixed herbs you can buy, into 50g/2oz/¼ cup soft butter. Take half a French stick (baguette) – white or brown – and cut it, as if you were going to slice it, but don't go right through the base. Butter the pieces generously on both sides, pulling them open to do so, then press them all together again. Wrap the loaf in foil and heat through in the hot oven for 15–20 minutes, until the butter has melted and the crust is crisp. Serve at once.

For a 1-person quantity, just mix a little butter with garlic, as described, and spread it on both sides of slices of bread. Heat the bread under the grill (broiler) until the butter has melted and the bread is slightly crisp on one side, then turn the bread over and grill (broil) the other side.

FREEZING AND REHEATING

All the soups will freeze; just put them into a suitable container and freeze them when they are cold. If you're short of containers, line a bowl or jug with a plastic bag or a layer of foil, pour the soup in and freeze; remove the bowl or jug when the soup is frozen. Secure the bag or arrange the foil so that the soup is completely covered; label.

When you want to use the soup, it's best to let it thaw out completely, which can take several hours, depending on the quantity, so remember to get the soup out of the freezer in good time. Then reheat the soup gently either in a saucepan on top of the stove, or in a bowl in a microwave. In the microwave it can take about 10 minutes, and it's helpful to give the mixture a stir once or twice, as the soup at the sides of the bowl gets hot before the soup in the middle.

carrot and ginger soup

This soup has a delicate flavour, smooth texture and beautiful colour, which make it suitable for serving as a first course for a special meal, yet it can be made for very little cost. Simply quarter or halve the ingredients if you're making it for one or two people, or double up for six or eight.

serves 4

Fry the onion gently in the butter in a large saucepan for 5 minutes, then add the potato, carrots, ginger and a sprinkling of salt. Fry for a further 10 minutes, with a lid on the pan, stirring from time to time. Add the water, bring up to the boil, then simmer gently for 15 minutes, or until the vegetables are cooked. Sieve the mixture, or whizz it in the food processor or blender then sieve. Return to the rinsed-out saucepan, reheat and season with salt and pepper. Top each bowlful with a spoonful of cream, if you're using this.

1 onion, peeled and chopped
15g/½oz/1tbsp butter
1 medium-sized potato,
peeled and cubed
450g/1lb carrots, scraped
and sliced
1tsp grated fresh ginger
sea salt
900ml/1½ pints/3¾ cups
water
freshly ground black pepper
4tbsp cream – optional

green lentil soup

This soup reheats well. Some hot garlic bread goes well with it. These quantities can be quartered or halved for one or two people and the cooking time remains the same.

serves 4

1 onion
1 celery stalk
1 carrot
1 sweet green pepper
1 medium-sized potato
1 clove garlic
½ tsp curry powder
½ tsp dried basil
225g/8oz/heaping 1 cup green lentils
1.5 litres/2½ pints/6¼ cups vegetable stock or water
400g/14oz can tomatoes
sea salt
freshly ground black pepper

Peel and chop the onion and chop the celery. Scrape and dice the carrot. Deseed and chop the green pepper. Peel and dice the potato and then crush the garlic.

Put all the ingredients into a large saucepan, bring to the boil, then simmer gently for about 40 minutes, until the lentils are tender. Season with sea salt and freshy ground black pepper.

golden lentil soup

Quite different from the soup opposite, this one is made from split red lentils. It is a satisfying, comforting soup, which makes an excellent cheap and filling main course with crusty wholewheat rolls or garlic bread. If you've got a pressure cooker, you can make it in about 10 minutes; even without, it can be made from start to finish in half an hour. Use a quarter or a half of these ingredients, and the same cooking time, for one or two people.

serves 4

Fry the onion in the butter in a saucepan or pressure cooker pan for 10 minutes, until tender but not browned. Add the lentils and stir for 1–2 minutes, then pour in the stock or water. Bring to the boil, then half cover the pan and leave the soup to simmer gently for 20 minutes, until the lentils are tender and pale-coloured. Or cook in the pressure cooker for 5 minutes. Beat the soup with a spoon to break up the lentils and make it smoother, or whizz in the food processor or blender. Add lemon juice and salt and pepper to taste.

1 large onion, chopped
15g/½oz/1tbsp butter
225g/8oz/heaping 1 cup split red lentils
1 litre/1¾ pints/1 quart vegetable stock or water
1–2tsp lemon juice
sea salt
freshly ground black pepper

potato and leek soup

This makes a thick, chunky soup, a real meal in itself on a cold day. For a lighter result, purée the soup and add enough extra water to make it the consistency you want. For real luxury, add a spoonful or two of cream and top with some chopped chives. Halve these quantities for one or two servings.

serves 4

25g/1oz/2tbsp butter
3 medium-sized leeks, washed and sliced
3 large potatoes, peeled and diced
3tsp vegetable broth powder
sea salt
freshly ground black pepper
1 litre/1¾ pints/1 quart water

Melt the butter in a large saucepan, then add the leeks and potatoes and fry these very gently, with a lid on the pan, for 10 minutes, stirring often. Sprinkle the broth powder and a little salt and pepper over the potatoes and leeks, stir, then continue to cook gently, still covered, for a further 10 minutes, stirring often. It doesn't matter if the vegetables brown slightly, but don't let them get too brown. Add the water, stir, then simmer for 5–10 minutes, until the vegetables are cooked. Check the seasoning.

potato and onion soup

This is an excellent variation. Replace the leeks with 2 large onions; peel, chop and fry with the potatoes.

lettuce soup

This is a soup which can be made for very little cost if you use the outer leaves of lettuce which you would otherwise throw away, or overgrown or very cheap lettuce when there's a glut. It's also good made with other green leaves such as spinach, sea kale and sorrel. It's quite filling, and with some wholewheat bread makes a good lunch. For special occasions it's extra good with some single (light) cream swirled on top of each bowlful. You need a food processor or blender for this one. Use a quarter of these quantities for one person, half for two, and the same cooking time.

makes 4 good bowlfuls

Fry the onion and potatoes in the butter in a large saucepan for 10 minutes, until they are beginning to soften but are not browned. Add the lettuce and cook for a further 2–3 minutes, then add the water. Bring up to the boil, then simmer for 15–20 minutes, until the potatoes are tender. Whizz in the food processor or blender, then return the soup to the rinsed-out saucepan. Season, reheat and serve.

1 onion, peeled and chopped
3 large potatoes, peeled and cut into even-sized pieces
25g/1oz/2tbsp butter
1 large cos lettuce or the equivalent in outer lettuce leaves, washed and roughly chopped
900ml/1½ pints/3¾ cups water
sea salt
freshly ground black pepper

french onion soup

This soup is very filling, and makes a good main course, followed by fruit or a light pudding. Halve these ingredients for one serving.

makes 2 large bowlfuls

15g/½oz/1tbsp butter
4 large onions, peeled and thinly sliced
sea salt
freshly ground black pepper
sugar
900ml/1½ pints/3¾ cups vegetable stock
1 clove garlic, crushed
a few drops of lemon juice
2 slices of French bread
50g/2oz/½ cup grated cheese

Melt the butter in a large saucepan and fry the onions for 10 minutes, until they're soft. Season with salt, pepper and about 2tsp sugar, then continue to fry for a further 10–15 minutes, until the onions are golden brown. Don't let them burn.

Add the stock, garlic and a few drops of lemon juice. Bring the soup to the boil and simmer for 10 minutes, then check the seasoning.

To serve the soup, put a piece of bread into each soup bowl and pour the soup on top. Sprinkle with grated cheese and grill (broil) until golden brown and melted. Serve immediately.

pistou

This easy-to-make, tasty and very filling bean soup from southern France makes a complete main course. If you're using dried beans, you need to allow time to soak and cook them beforehand. This soup reheats well. Make half these quantities for one or two people, and cook for the same amount of time.

serves 4

Fry the onion in the oil for 5 minutes, then add the drained beans, all the vegetables, garlic, some seasoning and the basil if you're using dried. Cook for 5 minutes, then add the stock and simmer for 20–30 minutes. Add the pasta and cook for a further 10 minutes. If you're using fresh basil, add this now; season to taste with salt and pepper.

1 onion, peeled and chopped
2tbsp oil – preferably olive oil
125g/4oz/heaping ½ cup haricot (navy) beans, soaked and cooked, or 400g/14oz can cannellini beans
2 carrots, scraped and diced
2 potatoes, peeled and diced
3 leeks or courgettes (zucchini), washed and sliced
400g/14oz can tomatoes
2 cloves garlic, crushed
sea salt
freshly ground black pepper
1tsp dried basil or 1–2tbsp torn fresh basil leaves
1 litre/1¾ pints/1 quart water or vegetable stock
50g/2oz thin pasta or pasta shapes

root vegetable soup

This is a tasty and economical winter soup. Serve it with warm wholewheat rolls or with some grated cheese sprinkled over the top if you want to make it into more of a meal. Use a quarter or a half of these quantities for one or two people, cooking for the same time.

serves 4

1.2 litres/2 pints/5 cups water
2 large carrots, scraped and sliced
2 onions, peeled and sliced
2 medium-sized potatoes, peeled and diced
about 225g/8oz/1¾ cups swede (rutabaga), peeled and diced
about 225g/8oz/1¾ cups turnip, peeled and diced
4 celery stalks, chopped
15g/½oz/1tbsp butter
sea salt
freshly ground black pepper

Pour the water into a large saucepan, add all the vegetables and bring to the boil. Simmer gently, with a lid on the saucepan, until all the vegetables are tender – about 30 minutes. Add the butter and mash some of the vegetables a bit, to thicken the soup, or whizz a cupful of the soup in the food processor or blender, then add to the remainder and reheat. Season to taste.

A béchamel or cheese sauce is quick to make and can turn a few vegetables, some hardboiled eggs or leftover cooked rice into a tasty meal. It's always useful to have some sauce in the fridge or the freezer, so it's worth making up more than you need. It will keep well in the fridge for 2–3 days, or for several weeks at least in the freezer.

Freeze the sauce in the portion size that you usually need. Clean yogurt or cottage cheese cartons make convenient containers, or you can use a plastic bag – open the bag and put it inside a jug to make it easier to fill.

To reheat, let the sauce thaw out for an hour or so, then reheat it gently in a saucepan on top of the stove, or in a non-metal bowl in the microwave, for about 5 minutes, stirring it several times.

basic béchamel sauce

This makes enough for 4 people, but the quantities can easily be halved. For one person, use 15g/½oz/1tbsp butter, 1tbsp flour and 150ml/5fl oz/⅔ cup milk.

makes 600ml/ 1 pint/2½ cups

600ml/1 pint/2½ cups milk
a piece of peeled onion
1 small carrot, scraped
a bayleaf
6 peppercorns
a few fresh parsley stems – if available
50g/2oz/¼ cup butter
2 rounded tbsp plain (all-purpose) flour
sea salt
freshly ground black pepper

Put the milk in a saucepan with the onion, carrot, bayleaf, peppercorns and parsley stems, if you have them. Bring to the boil, cover and set aside for 15 minutes. Then strain, reserving the milk. Melt the butter in the rinsed-out pan and stir in the flour. Cook for a moment or two, then add the milk. Stir over the heat until thickened. It will be lumpy at first, but as you stir and cook the lumps will disappear. If there are any obstinate ones, whisking the sauce will get rid of them. If you are adding the sauce to a dish which will have further cooking, add the seasoning and use the sauce as soon as it is thickened. If the sauce won't have further cooking, leave it to simmer over a low heat for 10 minutes, to cook the flour.

variations

Parsley sauce: add a couple of heaped tablespoons of chopped fresh parsley to the béchamel sauce.
Mushroom sauce: add 125g/4oz/1 cup finely chopped button mushrooms to the béchamel.
Cheese sauce: if you plan to use the sauce for a dish which will have further cooking, add 50–125g/2–4oz/½–1 cup grated cheese, 1tsp made mustard and salt and pepper to the béchamel as soon as it has thickened and you have taken it off the heat. If you are going to use the sauce without further cooking let it simmer for 10–15 minutes after thickening, then remove from the heat and add the cheese, mustard and seasoning.

tomato sauce

Tomato sauce is easy to make and, like cheese sauce and béchamel sauce, can be poured over cooked vegetables, sprinkled with crumbs and grated cheese, then baked, to make a tasty main course. It's also useful for serving with croquettes and other savoury dishes where some moisture and colour would make the meal more delicious and appetizing.

**makes about
300ml/10fl oz/
1¼ cups**

Fry the onion in the oil for 10 minutes, until tender but not browned. Then add the garlic and tomatoes and cook for 10–15 minutes, until thick. Season with salt and pepper. This sauce can be used as it is, or whizzed in the food processor or blender for a smoother texture.

1 onion, peeled and chopped
1tbsp oil
1 clove garlic, crushed
400g/14oz can tomatoes, chopped
sea salt
freshly ground black pepper

vegetarian gravy

I use soy sauce in my gravy, to darken as well as flavour it.

**makes about
300ml/10fl oz/
1¼ cups**

1 onion, peeled and chopped
1tbsp oil
1tbsp plain (all-purpose)
flour
1 clove garlic, crushed
300ml/10fl oz/1¼ cups
water
2–3tbsp soy sauce
1tsp yeast extract
sea salt
freshly ground black pepper

Fry the onion in the oil for 10 minutes, allowing it to brown a bit. Add the flour and cook until nut-brown in colour, then stir in the garlic and 300ml/10fl oz/1¼ cups water – or the water strained from cooked vegetables. Simmer for 5–10 minutes, to cook the flour, then add the soy sauce, yeast extract and salt and pepper to taste.

cauliflower, stilton and walnut bake

Strongly flavoured cheeses can work out quite cheap because you only need a little. This recipe works equally well if you halve or quarter the quantities, using a small cauliflower, or half a cauliflower.

Cook the cauliflower in 1cm/½ inch of boiling water for 4–5 minutes, then drain. Put the cauliflower in a lightly greased shallow ovenproof dish and sprinkle with the chopped walnuts.

Set the oven to 200°C/400°F/Gas 6 or preheat a moderate grill (broiler). Add the Stilton to the cheese sauce, then pour evenly over the cauliflower. Sprinkle the breadcrumbs and grated cheese over the top. Bake for 20–30 minutes, or put under the grill (broiler) for about 10 minutes, until the top is crispy and the inside hot and bubbly. Some watercress goes well with this, or sliced firm tomatoes, and either baked potatoes or crusty rolls.

1 large cauliflower, broken into florets
50g/2oz/½ cup walnut pieces, coarsely chopped
50–75g/2–3oz/½–¾ cup Stilton cheese, grated
600ml/1 pint/2½ cups cheese sauce – see page 12
4 heaped tbsp wholewheat breadcrumbs
4tbsp grated Cheddar-type cheese

easy mushrooms baked in cheese sauce

Very fast to make, and a wonderful way of serving those big open mushrooms. This recipe can easily be doubled for 4 people, or halved for one. Serve with hot wholewheat toast or some cooked rice.

serves 2

6–8 large open mushrooms
sea salt
freshly ground black pepper
300ml/10fl oz/1¼ cups
cheese sauce – see page 12

Set the oven to 200°C/400°F/Gas 6. Wash the mushrooms, then put them black-side up in a single layer in a lightly greased shallow ovenproof dish. Sprinkle them with salt and pepper, then spoon the sauce evenly over all the mushrooms. Bake for about 30 minutes, until the mushrooms are tender when pierced with a sharp knife and the sauce is browned on top and bubbling.

bread winners

Bread is wonderful as the basis of cheap, filling and speedy meals. As well as the bread-based dishes in this chapter, breadcrumbs feature in a number of recipes in other sections of this book.

Wholewheat breadcrumbs are both tasty and good for you. They are very easy to make, especially if you have a food processor or blender. To make crumbs, you need bread which is a day or two old. Cut off the crusts and crumble the bread between your fingers, or pop chunks of bread into the food processor or blender and whizz for a moment or two. It's worth making any leftover pieces of bread into crumbs and freezing them in a plastic bag. They can be used straight from the freezer.

Alternatively, you can dry out slices of bread in the bottom of the oven while something else is cooking, or in the microwave – they only take 5 minutes or so. Then crush them with a rolling pin or in the food processor. It's useful to have both fresh and dried breadcrumbs available.

mushroom and tomato layer

A savoury and delicious mixture; serve with a cooked vegetable, such as cauliflower. This works satisfactorily in a smaller quantity: halve or quarter the amounts to make enough for a double or single serving and bake for about 15 minutes only.

serves 4

50g/2oz/¼ cup butter
1 onion, peeled and finely chopped
12 heaped tbsp soft wholewheat breadcrumbs
125g/4oz/1 cup chopped nuts
1tsp dried mixed herbs
sea salt
freshly ground black pepper
225g/8oz/3 cups mushrooms, washed and chopped
450g/1lb tomatoes, peeled and chopped, or a 400g/14oz can, drained

Melt the butter in a medium-sized saucepan and fry the onion and breadcrumbs for about 10 minutes, until they're crisp. Remove from the heat and stir in the nuts and herbs, and seasoning to taste.

Set the oven to 200°C/400°F/Gas 6. Mix together the mushrooms and tomatoes; season with salt and pepper. Put a layer of one-third of the crumb mixture into an ovenproof dish and cover with half the mushroom mixture. Continue in layers, ending with the remaining crumb mixture. Bake in the oven for 30 minutes.

parsley burgers

Very cheap – and very good. A variation is to add some chopped black olives.

serves 1

Beat the eggs in a bowl, add the breadcrumbs, onion and parsley and season to taste. Pour enough oil into a frying pan to cover the base thinly and heat.

Form the parsley mixture into burgers and fry in the oil for about 3 minutes on both sides, until crisp. Drain on paper towels. Serve with salad.

2 eggs
6 heaped tbsp soft
wholewheat breadcrumbs
1 small onion, peeled and
finely chopped
4tbsp chopped fresh parsley
sea salt
freshly ground black pepper
oil for shallow frying

savoury bread and butter pudding

Made from simple everyday ingredients, this is very cheap and quick.

serves 1

3 slices of wholewheat bread

75–125g/3–4oz/¾–1 cup grated cheese

1 egg

150ml/5fl oz/⅔ cup milk

½ tsp mustard powder

sea salt

freshly ground black pepper

Set the oven to 200°C/400°F/Gas 6. Cut the slices of bread in half, and sandwich them using most of the cheese. Cut the cheese sandwiches into pieces and put them into a lightly greased shallow ovenproof dish. Whisk the egg with the milk, mustard powder and some salt and pepper to taste. Pour over the cheese sandwich pieces and sprinkle with the rest of the cheese. Bake in the oven for 20–30 minutes, until puffed up and golden brown. Serve at once. A tomato salad goes well with this.

easy cheese pudding

This is one step up from the last recipe, in terms of expense, interest, and the time it takes to make. Halve the ingredients for one serving.

serves 2–3

Set the oven to 200°C/400°F/Gas 6. Cut the slices of bread in half, and sandwich them together using most of the cheese. Cut the cheese sandwiches into pieces and put them into a lightly greased shallow ovenproof dish. Put the mushrooms, pepper and tomatoes into the dish on top of the cheese sandwiches, dotting them around. Whisk the eggs with the milk, mustard powder and some salt and pepper to taste. Pour over the cheese sandwich pieces and sprinkle with the rest of the cheese. Bake for 45 minutes, until puffed up and golden brown. Serve at once, with a cooked vegetable such as frozen peas, or a crisp salad.

3 slices of wholewheat bread
125g/4oz/1 cup grated cheese
125g/4oz/1½ cups mushrooms, washed and sliced
1 small sweet green pepper, deseeded and chopped
2 tomatoes, peeled and sliced
2 eggs
300ml/10fl oz/1¼ cups milk
1tsp mustard powder
sea salt
freshly ground black pepper

tomato bread pudding

The third step upwards in terms of cheese pudding/bake. It's not luxury food, but it's cheap, tasty and quite quick to make. For two portions, halve all the ingredients, but use 1 egg. Bake for 15–20 minutes.

serves 4

1 large onion
1 sweet green pepper
4 slices of wholewheat bread
25g/1oz/2tbsp butter
225g/8oz can tomatoes
1 heaped tbsp chopped fresh parsley
125g/4oz/1 cup grated cheese
1 egg
a few drops of Tabasco
sea salt
freshly ground black pepper
a little milk or water

Peel and chop the onion; deseed and chop the green pepper. Remove the crusts from the wholewheat bread. Set the oven to 190°C/ 375°F/Gas 5. Fry the onion and green pepper in the butter for 10 minutes. Meanwhile, mash the bread with the tomatoes, then add this to the onion mixture with the parsley, cheese, egg, Tabasco and salt and pepper to taste. Add a little milk or water if necessary to make a soft consistency. Spoon the mixture into a greased shallow dish and bake for 30 minutes.

toasted sandwiches

If you haven't got a sandwich toaster, toast two slices of bread on one side and put the filling on the untoasted sides. Grill (broil) until heated through, then sandwich together.

Cheese and tomato: thinly sliced or grated cheese and slices of tomato.

Cheese and onion: thinly sliced or grated cheese and a few thin slices of onion.

Cheese and pickle: thinly sliced or grated cheese mixed with some pickle or chutney.

Avocado: ripe avocado mashed and seasoned with salt and pepper. This is best done in a sandwich toaster, not under the grill (broiler).

Mushroom: chopped mushrooms, fried for a few minutes until tender. Allow 125g/4oz/1½ cups for each sandwich.

Tomato and garlic: allow 2 peeled and chopped tomatoes and a crushed clove garlic for each sandwich.

cheese on toast

serves 1

Preheat the grill (broiler). Toast the bread on one side. Blend the cheese to a paste with the milk and season with some pepper. Spread on the untoasted side of the bread and grill (broil) until puffed up and golden brown.

1–2 slices of wholewheat bread
75–125g/3–4oz/¾–1 cup grated cheese
1–2tbsp milk
freshly ground black pepper

bread pizza

This is a quick way of making a pizza, and it's very good. These quantities make enough for two hungry people. For one person, simply halve – or quarter – all the ingredients.

serves 2–4

1 round or oval wholewheat loaf, weighing about 450g/1lb
olive oil
2 large onions, peeled and sliced
2 cloves garlic, crushed
400g/14oz can tomatoes, chopped
dried oregano
sea salt
freshly ground black pepper
125g/4oz/1 cup grated cheese
8 black olives

Set the oven to 220°C/425°F/Gas 7. Cut the loaf in half horizontally and scoop out some of the crumbs. Brush inside and outside the halved loaf with oil and place on a baking sheet. Fry the onions in 1tbsp oil for 10 minutes, then add the garlic and fry for a further minute or two. Remove from the heat and add the tomatoes, a little oregano, and salt and pepper to taste. Spoon the tomato mixture on to the bread halves, sprinkle with the grated cheese and dot with the olives. Bake for 15 minutes. Serve with a green salad.

Cheese is a useful and very economical budget food. When I refer to cheese in a recipe, I mean an ordinary inexpensive Cheddar-type, though it can be a saving to buy a more expensive, well-flavoured variety, such as a matured farmhouse Cheddar, because you need much less, and so it goes further. Cheese is included in dishes in other sections in this book; the ones which follow are those which have cheese as their main ingredient.

choose cheese

cheese dip

This is quick to make and, with some sticks of carrot and celery to dip into it, makes a nourishing snack, or a light lunch or supper, perhaps following a soup such as the lettuce soup on page 7. For a packed lunch, put the dip into a small container such as a yogurt pot. The mixture is quite rich, so a little goes a long way.

serves 2–4

40g/1½oz/3tbsp soft butter
150g/5oz/1¼ cups cheese, grated fairly finely
6tbsp milk
1–2 drops of Tabasco
sea salt
freshly ground black pepper

To garnish
a little paprika pepper or a sprig of parsley – if available

Put the butter into a bowl and beat until creamy, then gradually beat in the grated cheese and milk, to make a thick, creamy mixture. Add the Tabasco and a little seasoning. Spoon the mixture into a small dish to serve. It looks pretty with a sprinkling of mild red paprika pepper or a small sprig of parsley on top, if you have it.

cheese fondue

Cheese fondue is quick to make and always seems rather special and festive. It can be quite cheap – and very good – when made with Edam cheese and dry cider. You don't need lots of special equipment: an ordinary saucepan will do, though it's quite nice – but not essential – to have a table candle burner if one is available, to keep the fondue hot while you dip in your bread. These quantities can be halved for a one-person serving.

serves 2

Rub the garlic around the inside of a medium-sized saucepan. Discard the garlic. Put 6tbsp cider into the pan and bring just to the boil, then add the cheese and stir over a gentle heat until the cheese has melted. Mix the cornflour (cornstarch) with the remaining tablespoonful of cider and add to the cheese mixture. Stir until slightly thickened. Remove from the heat and add the lemon juice. Season with salt, pepper and nutmeg.

To eat, place the pan of fondue in the middle of the table, and use long forks to spear pieces of bread and dip them into the fondue.

1 clove garlic, halved
7tbsp dry cider
225g/8oz/2 cups Edam cheese, grated
1tsp cornflour (cornstarch)
½ tsp lemon juice
sea salt
freshly ground black pepper
grated nutmeg

To serve
1 French stick (baguette), white or brown, cut into bite-sized pieces and warmed in the oven

glamorgan sausages

Quick to make, crisp little sausages which are good with a cooked vegetable or a salad. Halve the quantities for one person: double them for four.

serves 2–3

125g/4oz/1 cup grated cheese

soft breadcrumbs made from 4–5 slices of wholewheat bread, crusts removed

1tbsp finely grated onion

1tbsp chopped fresh parsley

1tsp made mustard

sea salt

freshly ground black pepper

To finish

1 egg, beaten, or a few tbsp milk

dried breadcrumbs

oil for shallow frying

To make the sausages, mix all the ingredients together. If the mixture seems very stiff, add 1tbsp water. It should be firm enough to shape. Form the mixture into small sausages, dip them in beaten egg or milk, then into dried crumbs. Pour a little oil into a frying pan, to cover the base thinly, and heat. Put in the sausages and fry them, turning them with a palette knife (metal spatula) so that they get crisp and browned all over. Drain on paper towels. Serve immediately.

deep-fried camembert

The crisp coating makes a delightful contrast with the hot runny cheese inside. Serve with a fresh salad: a green one, or tomato and onion, and something sweet, like mango or apricot chutney. Halve the quantities for one person, and omit the tablespoonful of water.

**serves 2 well or
3 at a pinch**

Dip the pieces of Camembert into the egg, then into the crumbs or wheatgerm, to coat well. Have your deep frying oil so that it fills no more than a third of the pan. Heat the oil to 190°C/375°F, or so that a small cube of bread sizzles immediately it's thrown in and becomes golden brown in 1 minute. Put in the pieces of Camembert and fry for 4–5 minutes, until they are crisp and golden brown. Remove them with a slotted spoon and put them on crumpled paper towels. Serve immediately.

1 box of Camembert – choose the type which has 6 individual triangles in it
1 egg, beaten with 1tbsp water
dried crumbs or wheatgerm, for coating
oil for deep frying

egg cheese pie

Serve with a cooked green vegetable, or grilled (broiled) tomatoes, or frozen peas or beans. For two people, halve the quantities; for one, quarter them. Bake these smaller pies for about 20 minutes. If there's any over, mix it together, form into croquettes, coat with beaten egg and crumbs, and fry until crisp on both sides. Nice with a crisp lettuce salad.

serves 4

6 hardboiled eggs, shelled and chopped

For the potato topping
2–3 large potatoes, peeled and cut into even-sized pieces
15g/½oz/1tbsp butter
1–2tbsp milk

For the sauce
50g/2oz/¼ cup butter
2 heaped tbsp plain (all-purpose) flour
600ml/1 pint/2½ cups milk
125g/4oz/1 cup grated cheese
½tsp ground mace – optional
sea salt
freshly ground black pepper

Start by making the potato topping. Put the potatoes into a saucepan, cover with cold water and bring to the boil. Boil until the potatoes are tender, about 20 minutes.

While the potatoes are cooking, set the oven to 190°C/375°F/Gas 5 and make a cheese sauce. Put the butter, flour and milk into a saucepan and whisk over a moderate heat until thickened. Remove from the heat and add the cheese, the mace if using, and salt and pepper to taste. Add the hardboiled eggs, then pour the mixture into a shallow ovenproof dish.

Drain the potatoes and dry them in the pan over the heat for a minute or two, then mash them with the butter and add enough milk to make a creamy consistency. Season with salt and pepper.

Spoon the mashed potato evenly over the cheese sauce and mark the top with a fork. Bake for 30 minutes, until browned on top.

Eggs are one of the great convenience foods. A boiled, scrambled or poached egg, or an omelette, makes a very quick and nutritious meal. Here are variations on the egg theme, all quick and easy to make.

I suggest free-range eggs in the recipes; they do cost a little more, but it's good to feel that they were laid by happy hens and they've also been shown to contain a little more vitamin B12.

To hardboil eggs – needed for several of these recipes – put the eggs into a saucepan and cover with cold water. Bring to the boil, then let the eggs simmer gently for 10 minutes. Drain off the water, then cover with cold water. Crack the shells by tapping the eggs sharply all over, then ease off the shell with your fingers and rinse the eggs under the cold tap to remove any small pieces of shell. A tip for preventing the eggs boiling out of their shells, which sometimes seems to happen however careful you are, is to put three or four used matchsticks into the water with the eggs. I don't know why this works, but it does.

Don't ever attempt to hardboil eggs in a microwave oven – they explode.

pipérade

This French version of scrambled eggs with vegetables makes a delicious and economical supper dish in the late summer when tomatoes and peppers are cheap. It's an excellent dish for one: just halve the ingredients.

serves 2

1 large onion, peeled and chopped
25g/1oz/2tbsp butter
1 large sweet green pepper, deseeded and chopped
450g/1lb tomatoes, peeled and chopped
1–2 cloves garlic, crushed
4 eggs, beaten
sea salt
freshly ground black pepper

To serve
hot crusty rolls or fingers of wholewheat toast

Fry the onion in the butter for 10 minutes, until it is soft but not browned, then add the green pepper, tomatoes and garlic and cook gently, without a lid on the pan, for a further 15–20 minutes, until the vegetables are soft but not mushy.

Pour in the beaten eggs and stir gently until the eggs begin to set. Remove from the heat – the eggs will continue to cook in the heat of the vegetables – and stir in some salt and pepper to taste. Serve with hot rolls or fingers of toast.

baked eggs

A very easy, delicious and cheap supper dish, baked eggs can be varied according to what ingredients you have available. For each baked egg, allow a little butter, a little cooked mushroom, onion, sweet pepper or another vegetable, a spoonful of milk or cream and a little grated cheese.

serves 1

Set the oven to 190°C/375°F/Gas 5. Put the cooked vegetables into greased little ovenproof dishes or ramekins and stand these in a baking pan containing hot water. Break a free-range egg into each dish, spoon over the milk or cream, season with salt and pepper and sprinkle with grated cheese. Bake for 15–20 minutes, until the eggs are set. Serve immediately, with hot wholewheat toast.

variation

For baked eggs in tomatoes, put all the ingredients into a large beefsteak tomato which has had the inside scooped out and sprinkled with salt and pepper. Bake as described, until the egg is set and the tomato lightly cooked.

cheese soufflé

serves 4

25g/1oz/2tbsp butter
1 heaped tbsp plain
(all-purpose) flour
150ml/5fl oz/⅔ cup milk
½ tsp mustard powder
125g/4oz/1 cup grated
cheese
4 eggs, separated
sea salt
freshly ground black pepper

Set the oven to 180°C/350°F/Gas 4. Melt the butter in a saucepan and stir in the flour. Mix for a moment or two, then add the milk and stir over the heat until thickened. Remove from the heat and beat in the mustard and cheese. Leave to cool slightly, then beat in the egg yolks and seasoning. Whisk the egg whites until stiff but not so stiff you could slice them with a knife. Stir a couple of tablespoonfuls of egg white into the cheese mixture to lighten it. Using a metal spoon, fold in the rest. Turn into a greased soufflé dish – a 1 litre/1¾ pint/ 1 quart one is perfect, but any medium-sized ovenproof dish will do – and level the top. Bake for 40–45 minutes, until the soufflé is puffed up and doesn't wobble when you shake it. Serve immediately.

variations

Individual cheese soufflés: bake the mixture in 4 small ovenproof dishes or ramekins for 15–20 minutes.
Cheese soufflé for one: follow the method above, using 15g/½oz/1tbsp butter, 1½tsp flour, 4tbsp milk, a pinch of mustard, 25g/1oz/¼ cup grated cheese, 1 egg and salt and pepper to taste. Bake for 15 minutes.
Cheese soufflé tomatoes: slice the tops off 4 large beefsteak tomatoes and scoop out the pulp. Sprinkle the insides with salt and leave upside down. Make the soufflé mixture. Place the tomatoes in a dish, fill with soufflé and replace the tops. Bake for 15–20 minutes.

egg cutlets

For one person, simply halve the ingredients.

Beat the eggs in a bowl and add the breadcrumbs, chopped onion, hardboiled eggs and parsley; season to taste. Pour enough oil into a frying pan to cover the base thinly and heat. Form the parsley mixture into burgers and fry in the oil for about 3 minutes on both sides, until crisp. Drain on paper towels. Serve with a salad.

2 eggs
6 heaped tbsp soft
wholewheat breadcrumbs
1 small onion, peeled and
finely chopped
2 hardboiled eggs, shelled
and chopped
4tbsp chopped fresh parsley
sea salt
freshly ground black pepper
oil for shallow frying

spanish omelette

These quantities can be halved for one person.

serves 2

2tbsp olive oil
1 onion, peeled and chopped
1 carrot, peeled and coarsely grated
1 small sweet green pepper, deseeded and chopped
225g/8oz/2 cups courgettes (zucchini), diced
1–2 cloves garlic, crushed
4 eggs, beaten
sea salt
freshly ground black pepper

Heat the oil in a large frying pan and fry the onion, carrot and green pepper, uncovered, for 5 minutes. Add the courgettes (zucchini) and cook for a further 5 minutes.

Preheat the grill (broiler). Add the garlic, beaten eggs and some seasoning to the vegetables and stir gently until the omelette begins to set. When the omelette is set underneath, place it under the grill (broiler) to set the top, but don't let it get too hard. Cut in two and serve.

Batter, quickly made from storecupboard ingredients, is a useful standby in the thrifty cook's repertoire, and found in various forms in many of the cuisines of the world. Yorkshire pudding has long been used to eke out the expensive Sunday roast – and is nourishing enough to stand on its own, with vegetables, roast potatoes and tasty gravy. Crêpes, too, make a nourishing meal, either with sweet or savoury fillings.

Old-wives' tales have it that batter has to stand for an hour or so before you use it – personally, I ignore them. I've found that it's just as good when cooked straight away.

better batter

mushroom toad-in-the-hole

This is delicious made with field mushrooms, should you be able to lay your hands on some. Otherwise choose the largest and most open mushrooms you can find. Use a baking pan to cook this in rather than a casserole dish because the metal conducts the heat better and makes the batter puffy and crisp. For two people, halve all the ingredients and bake for 25–30 minutes; for one person, use 1 egg, 4tbsp milk and a quarter of all the other ingredients. Bake for 15–20 minutes.

serves 4

225g/8oz open mushrooms or field mushrooms
4tbsp oil
125g/4oz/¾ cup + 2tbsp plain wholewheat flour or a half-and-half mix of plain white (all-purpose) flour and wholewheat flour
½tsp salt
2 eggs
300ml/10fl oz/1¼ cups milk

Preheat the oven to 220°C/425°F/Gas 7. Wash the mushrooms and peel them if you're using field ones. Cut into even-sized pieces. Heat 2tbsp of the oil in a saucepan and fry the mushrooms for 2–3 minutes on each side. Drain.

Put the flour and salt into a large bowl, make a well in the middle and break in the eggs. Add half the milk and mix well, gradually mixing in all the flour and adding the rest of the milk. Put the remaining 2tbsp oil into a baking pan and heat in the oven until smoking hot, then pour in the batter and pop the mushrooms in on top. Bake for 35 minutes, until puffed up and golden brown. A tasty gravy, mashed potatoes and a cooked vegetable such as cabbage or carrots go well with this. I also think it's nice with a crisp green salad.

savoury olive mushroom cake

This recipe was given to me by a French friend. If, like me, you like olives, you'll love it. A half quantity of this also works well, baked for about 30 minutes, for two people, as does a quarter quantity, baked in a small dish or pan for 15–20 minutes, for one person. If you haven't any leftover white wine, water will do, but the wine gives a subtle fruity flavour.

serves 4

Set the oven to 250°C/500°F/Gas 9. Grease a cake or bread pan. Put the flour and salt into a bowl and add the eggs, wine and oil. Mix until smooth, then add the olives, mushrooms and grated cheese. Spoon the mixture into the prepared pan. Bake for 10 minutes, then turn the oven setting down to 190°C/375°F/Gas 5 and bake for a further 40–45 minutes.

275g/10oz/2 cups self-raising wholewheat flour or a half-and-half mix of white and wholewheat self-raising flour
pinch of salt
4 eggs
150ml/5fl oz/²⁄₃ cup white wine
4tbsp olive oil
225g/8oz/1¹⁄₃ cups stoned (pitted) green olives
175g/6oz/2¹⁄₄ cups sliced mushrooms
175g/6oz/1¹⁄₂ cups grated cheese

crêpes

These quantities can easily be halved to make the right amount for one or two people.

125g/4oz/¾ cup + 2tbsp
plain wholewheat flour or a
half-and-half mix of plain
white (all-purpose) flour
and wholewheat flour
½ tsp salt
2 eggs
150ml/5fl oz/⅔ cup milk
150ml/5fl oz/⅔ cup water
2tbsp melted butter
extra butter for frying

Put the flour and salt into a bowl, mix in the eggs, then gradually add the milk, water and butter to make a smooth, fairly thin batter. Heat 7g/¼oz/½tbsp butter in a small frying pan; when it sizzles, pour off the excess, so the pan is just glistening. Keep the pan over a high heat, give the batter a quick stir, then put 2 tablespoonfuls into the pan and tip it to make it run all over the base. Cook the crêpe for about 30 seconds, until the top is set and the underneath is tinged golden brown, then quickly flip the crêpe over to cook the other side. Remove with a palette knife (metal spatula) and put it on to a plate. Repeat to make about a dozen crêpes in all, piling them up on top of each other on the plate.

sweet ideas

Sugar and lemon: sprinkle crêpes with sugar and serve with lemon wedges.

Honey or syrup: pour warmed honey, golden syrup or maple syrup over the crêpes and serve with lemon wedges.

Chocolate crêpes: replace 1tbsp of the flour in the batter with 1tbsp cocoa powder. Serve with whipped cream.

Fruity filling: spread the crêpes with stewed apples, rhubarb or other fruit – see page 144; sprinkle with sugar and serve with yogurt or cream if you like.

savoury suggestions

Crêpes can be filled and served as they are, or filled, covered with a cheese or tomato sauce and grated cheese, then baked in a 190°C/375°F/Gas 5 oven. Allow 45 minutes for a 4-person quantity, 30 minutes for a 2-person bake, and 15–20 minutes for one. These quantities are enough to fill crêpes for 4 people.

Spinach: wash 900g/2lb fresh spinach. Remove and chop the stems; roughly chop the leaves. Heat 6mm/¼ inch of water in a saucepan and put in the stems. Boil for 4–5 minutes, until stems are nearly tender, then drain off the water and put in the leaves. Cook for 5–8 minutes, until the leaves are tender. Drain well. Add butter, salt, pepper and nutmeg to taste. Spinach crêpes are good served with cheese sauce.

Red kidney bean and tomato: fry a chopped onion in 25g/1oz/2tbsp butter for 10 minutes, then add a 400g/14oz can tomatoes, a crushed clove of garlic and the drained contents of a 400g/14oz can red kidney beans. Season and cook until heated through.

Mushroom: fry a chopped onion in 25g/1oz/2tbsp butter for 10 minutes, add 450g/1lb/6 cups chopped mushrooms and cook for 3–4 minutes. Add 2 peeled and chopped tomatoes, heat gently and season with salt, pepper and nutmeg.

Ratatouille: follow the recipe on page 67.

Sweetcorn: cook 450g/1lb/2¼ cups fresh or frozen sweetcorn in boiling water, drain and add 150ml/5fl oz/⅔ cup soured cream or cheese sauce to bind. Season.

Potato and pea: mix 450g/1lb/3 cups diced boiled potatoes and 125g/4oz/scant 1 cup peas with a chopped and fried onion. A tablespoonful of grated fresh ginger is good in this.

savoury brazil nut fritters

Easy to make, cheap, savoury and delicious, these puffed-up fritters are delicious with gravy and cooked vegetables, or with a sauce made by stirring some chopped chives, onion or lightly fried sliced button mushrooms into some soured cream or plain yogurt. They're also good with chutney. For two people, use a whole egg and about 4tbsp milk; halve all the other ingredients. For one person, make a two-person quantity, and freeze or keep half.

serves 4

125g/4oz/¾ cup + 2 tbsp self-raising wholewheat flour or a half-and-half mix of white and wholewheat self-raising flour
1 egg
150ml/5fl oz/⅔ cup milk
100g/4oz/1 cup Brazil nuts, roughly chopped
1 small onion, peeled and finely chopped
1 clove garlic, crushed
½ tsp dried mixed herbs
2tbsp chopped fresh parsley – if available
sea salt
freshly ground black pepper
oil for shallow frying

Put the flour into a bowl and add the egg and milk. Beat well to make a smooth batter, then add the nuts, onion, garlic, dried mixed herbs, parsley if you've got it, and seasoning to taste. Pour enough oil into a frying pan to cover the base very thinly, and put over a moderate heat. When it's really hot, drop tablespoonfuls of the batter into the frying pan, leaving a little room for them to spread. When the underside is lightly browned and bubbles are rising to the surface, flip the fritters over with a palette knife (metal spatula) and cook the other side. Drain on paper towels. Serve when they are all done.

The all-time favourite 'fast food', as long as it isn't overcooked, pasta is good almost any way. A big bowlful of pasta served with just butter, crushed garlic, sea salt and freshly ground black pepper, and a sprinkling of Parmesan if the budget allows, makes a comforting meal when you're very hard up, and it's nourishing, filling and high in fibre. It's interesting to try the different shapes, and sometimes to mix green and white pasta, perhaps intensifying the colour contrast by stirring in some chopped fresh dark green herbs, too. And leftover pasta can be made into a good salad.

If you like sauce with your pasta, it's a good idea to make up a double batch of a favourite, such as the fresh tomato, or the lentil and herb, and store half of it in the fridge or freezer for another day.

The first essential is to use your largest saucepan, because pasta needs to be able to move around in the water so that it doesn't stick together and come out in a solid mass. Fill the pan two thirds full with water and bring to the boil. When the water reaches a rolling boil, throw in some salt and your pasta, or, if it's spaghetti, hold it in your hand like a bunch of flowers, stand the base of the 'stems' in the water and gently push them down into the water as they soften, until it's all in. Then give the pasta a quick stir and let it boil away, without a lid, until it's done. This will take anything from about 7 to 15 minutes, depending on the size of the pieces. The packet will give a guide, but fish a piece of pasta out with a slotted spoon and bite it just before the time is up, to see how it's doing. It should be tender but nowhere near soggy. As soon as it reaches this stage, drain it. The easiest way to do this is to use a metal colander, stand it squarely in the sink and pour all the pasta and water into it. Give the colander a good shake to dislodge all the water, then pop the pasta back into the saucepan and add a piece of butter and some sea salt and freshly ground black pepper. Serve at once, before it has a chance to cool down, as it is, or with any trimmings you may have.

If you're serving pasta as a main meal, without much else, two hungry people will probably happily get through 350g/12oz; otherwise, allow 175–250g/6–8oz for two.

SIMPLE ADDITIONS FOR PASTA

You can turn hot cooked pasta into a feast very simply by adding other ingredients.

Pasta with fresh herbs: just add a tablespoonful or so of chopped or torn fresh herbs to the buttery cooked pasta. Tarragon and basil are especially delicious.
Creamy pasta: stir a little double (heavy) cream into the hot cooked pasta, allowing a couple of tablespoonfuls per person. This is a luxury-tasting dish, but it isn't nearly as fatty as it sounds when you consider how much cheese people often put over their pasta.
Cheesy pasta: sprinkle the pasta with a little dry grated cheese: Cheddar which has been left uncovered in the fridge or cupboard to dry out, for rock-bottom prices; Parmesan if you can afford it. Parmesan is nicest if you can buy a small piece and keep it in the fridge to grate as you need it. Grate it on the fine side of the grater; it's very hard, and is expensive, but a little goes a long way.

Pasta with avocado: a small ripe avocado, peeled and chopped, added to the hot cooked pasta after draining, will heat through a little in the heat of the pasta. The buttery flavour and texture of avocado go well with pasta.

Pasta with nuts: a few chopped, very fresh, walnuts go beautifully with hot cooked pasta. They're nicest if you buy them in the shell and crack a few while the pasta cooks. Chop them roughly and add to the drained and buttered pasta. A little cream mixed in as well makes this really special.

Pasta with beans and black olives: while the pasta is cooking, heat through a can of cannellini beans in another saucepan. Drain both the beans and the pasta and mix together with a little crushed garlic, a tablespoonful or so of olive oil and a few whole black olives. If you want to be even more elaborate, you can add a peeled and chopped tomato and some chopped fresh parsley.

Pasta with chick peas: an old Italian favourite, this is just hot drained chick peas (garbanzo beans), either canned or home cooked, added to hot cooked pasta with some olive oil to make the whole lot glossy, and plenty of crushed garlic.

Pasta with croûtons: while the pasta is cooking, cut a slice of wholewheat bread for each person, cut off the crusts, and cut the bread into 6mm/¼ inch squares. Heat a little olive oil in a frying pan and fry the bread croûtons until crisp and golden brown all over. Drain on paper towels. Add the croûtons to each bowl of hot pasta.

Pasta with onions: start this when you put the water for the pasta on to boil, to give the onions time to cook until they're really soft and slightly caramelized. For each person, allow ½–1 large onion, peeled and sliced. Heat a piece of butter in a frying pan and put in the onion. Fry for 10 minutes, then add a sprinkling of salt, pepper and sugar, and continue to fry for a further 5–10 minutes, until the onion is golden brown but not burnt. Stir the hot cooked onion into the cooked and drained pasta.

PASTA FOR SAUCES

One step up from just adding tasty ingredients to cooked pasta is to make a sauce to pour on top of it. This needn't be a complicated affair: the tomato sauce, the tomato and mushroom sauce and the creamy mushroom sauce can all be made while the pasta cooks.

Fresh tomato sauce: allow about a tablespoonful of finely chopped onion and 2 good-sized tomatoes for each person. Peel and chop the tomatoes. Fry the onion in a piece of butter in a medium-sized pan for 5 minutes, then put in the tomatoes and a crushed clove of garlic and fry gently for 5 minutes or so, until both the tomatoes and the onion are tender. Season with salt and pepper. Serve this as it is, poured over the hot cooked pasta, or whizz in the food processor or blender first. If you're making this for two, and want to make it more cheaply, you can use a 400g/14oz can tomatoes. They don't taste so fresh, but are fine if well flavoured with the onion and garlic.

Fresh tomato and mushroom sauce: make in the same way as the above, adding 25–50g/1–2oz/⅓–⅔ cup washed and finely chopped button mushrooms with the tomatoes.

Mushroom sauce: allow 125g/4oz/1½ cups mushrooms for each person. Wash and chop the mushrooms, then fry them lightly in a little butter for 4–5 minutes, until tender. Add 2tbsp soured cream, plain yogurt or double (heavy) cream, some salt, pepper and crushed garlic, and freshly grated nutmeg if you have it.

Nutty sauce: you need a food processor or blender or some patience with a pestle and mortar for this one. For two servings, crush 1 clove garlic, then add 50g/2oz/⅔ cup walnuts – or pine nuts, if you're feeling extravagant – and a pinch each of dried thyme, salt, pepper and sugar. When it's all fairly smooth and thick, gradually mix in 2–3tbsp milk or cream. Add this to the hot cooked pasta and mix with a fork so that the sauce coats all the pasta, then serve.

tagliatelle with lentil sauce

This sauce takes a bit longer to make than the sauces on the opposite page, but is cheap, tasty and turns cooked tagliatelle into a very filling, welcoming meal. For one or two people, halve the ingredients, using a 225g/8oz can tomatoes. For one, it's probably best to make a half quantity and freeze what you don't need, or keep it in the fridge for a day or two for another meal.

serves 4

Start making the sauce. Fry the onion in the oil for 10 minutes, then add the garlic, cinnamon, lentils, tomatoes and water and bring up to the boil. Let the mixture simmer gently for about 20 minutes, until the lentils are tender; taste and season with salt and pepper. While the lentil sauce is cooking, cook the tagliatelle as described on page 44. Put the cooked tagliatelle in a warmed large serving dish and pour the sauce into the middle. Offer grated cheese separately.

225–350g/8–12oz
tagliatelle – green or white
15g/½ oz/1tbsp butter
grated cheese, to serve

For the sauce
1 large onion, peeled and
chopped
2tbsp oil
2 cloves garlic, crushed
½ tsp ground cinnamon
225g/8oz/heaping 1 cup
split red lentils, washed
400g/14oz can tomatoes
400ml/14fl oz/1¾ cups
water
sea salt
freshly ground black pepper

spaghetti with green lentils and tomatoes

Halve these quantities for one person.

serves 3

225–350g/8–12oz spaghetti
15g/½oz/1tbsp butter
grated cheese, to serve

For the sauce
125g/4oz/heaping ½ cup
green lentils
15g/½oz/1tbsp butter
1 large onion, peeled and
chopped
1 clove garlic, crushed
1tsp dried basil or 1tbsp
torn fresh basil
225g/8oz/1¼ cups
tomatoes, peeled and
chopped, or a 225g/8oz can
sea salt
freshly ground black pepper

First make the sauce. Put the lentils into a large saucepan with water to cover generously and boil gently until tender, 45–60 minutes. Drain.

Melt the butter in a large saucepan and fry the onion until tender. Add the garlic, basil if you're using dried, tomatoes and drained lentils. Season with salt and pepper. While the lentil sauce is cooking, cook the spaghetti as described on page 44. Reheat the sauce, adding the basil if you're using fresh. Put the cooked spaghetti in a warmed large serving dish and pour the sauce into the middle. Offer grated cheese separately.

macaroni cheese

An always popular old favourite, with a tangy sauce. These quantities will halve satisfactorily to make enough for two people; for one person, use 50g/2oz/²/₃ cup macaroni, 15g/½oz/1tbsp butter, 2 rounded tsp flour, 200ml/7fl oz/scant 1 cup milk, ½tsp mustard and 40g/1½oz/⅓ cup grated cheese.

serves 4

Fill a large saucepan three quarters full of water, bring to the boil and add 1tsp salt. Then add the macaroni, stir, and cook for 8–10 minutes, without a lid on the pan, until the macaroni is just tender.

While the macaroni is cooking, preheat the grill (broiler) or set the oven to 200°C/400°F/Gas 6, and make the sauce. Melt the butter in a saucepan, add the flour and stir for a moment or two over the heat. Then stir in the milk, a quarter at a time, stirring well and allowing the sauce to thicken between each lot of milk. Simmer gently for 5 minutes, remove from the heat and add the mustard, two thirds of the cheese and salt and pepper to taste.

Drain the macaroni, add to the sauce and stir well. Spoon into a large shallow ovenproof dish. Sprinkle the crumbs and the remaining cheese over the top. Grill (broil) for 5–10 minutes, or heat through in the oven for about 20 minutes, until the top is golden brown and crisp and the inside bubbling. Serve with a crisp salad.

sea salt
225g/8oz/2²/₃ cups macaroni
50g/2oz/¼ cup butter
2 rounded tbsp plain (all-purpose) flour
900ml/1½ pints/3¾ cups milk
2tsp made mustard
175g/6oz/1½ cups grated cheese
freshly ground black pepper
6 heaped tbsp wholewheat breadcrumbs

macaroni bake

This is tasty, can be prepared in advance for baking later, and also freezes well. Some cooked frozen peas go well with it or a crisp green salad. For two servings, halve all the ingredients but use a whole egg. Make this quantity for one, and freeze what you don't need, or keep the remainder in the fridge for another day, perhaps as a stuffing for a sweet green pepper – prepared as on page 82, stuffed, then baked for 15 minutes.

serves 4

sea salt
125g/4oz/1⅓ cups macaroni
1tbsp oil
2 onions, peeled and chopped
125g/4oz/1½ cups mushrooms, washed and chopped
225g/8oz/1¼ cups tomatoes, peeled and chopped
1 egg, beaten
125g/4oz/1 cup grated cheese
freshly ground black pepper
a few wholewheat breadcrumbs, for topping

Fill a large saucepan two-thirds full of water, bring to the boil and add 1tsp salt. Then put in the macaroni, stir, and let it simmer, without a lid on the pan, for 8–10 minutes, until a piece feels just tender when you bite it.

While the macaroni is cooking, set the oven to 190°C/375°F/Gas 5. Heat the oil in a saucepan and fry the onions for 7 minutes, then add the mushrooms and tomatoes and cook for a further 3 minutes. Beat in the egg and stir over the heat for a moment or two longer until the egg begins to set. Remove from the heat.

Drain the macaroni immediately it is done. The easiest way to do this is to pour it into a metal colander. Add the macaroni and grated cheese to the vegetable mixture and season to taste with some salt and pepper, then spoon the mixture into a shallow ovenproof dish. Sprinkle crumbs over the top and bake for 25–30 minutes, until the top is crisp and golden brown.

pasta with leeks and cheese

An easy pasta dish which can be made in a quarter or half portion for one or two people.

serves 4

Fill a large saucepan two thirds full of water, bring to the boil and add 1tsp salt. Then put in the pasta rings, stir, and let them simmer, without a lid on the pan, for about 10 minutes, until a piece of pasta feels just tender when you bite it.

While the pasta is cooking, prepare the leeks. To do this, pour 1cm/½ inch of water into a saucepan and when it boils, put in the leeks. Boil for 4–5 minutes, until just tender, then drain well. Preheat the grill (broiler) and grease the grill (broiler) pan or a shallow flameproof dish which will fit under the grill (broiler).

Drain the pasta immediately it is done and put it into the prepared pan or dish in an even layer. Put the leeks on top and season with some pepper. Sprinkle the cheese over the top and grill (broil) until the cheese has melted and is golden brown. Serve immediately. A tomato salad goes well with this.

sea salt
225g/8oz/2⅔ cups
wholewheat pasta rings
4 leeks, trimmed, washed
and cut into 1cm/½ inch
pieces
freshly ground black pepper
175g/6oz/1½ cups grated
cheese

pasta salads

These are a good way of using up some leftover cooked pasta, but they're also worth making specially, because they make a pleasant filling meal. Just add some vinaigrette, cream, plain yogurt or mayonnaise to the cooked pasta, then put in some colourful and varied ingredients to make the salad tasty and interesting.

Macaroni and tomato salad: cooked macaroni, black olives, finely chopped onion and chopped peeled tomatoes, dressed with some vinaigrette.

Pasta shells with carrot and raisins: cooked, well-drained pasta shells mixed with coarsely grated carrots and some raisins, with mayonnaise, yogurt or soured cream to bind. Some cooked sweetcorn kernels are good in this, too, instead of, or as well as, the raisins.

Two-colour pasta and herb salad: cook equal quantities of green and white pasta twists; drain well. Dress with vinaigrette and add plenty of chopped fresh herbs.

Nutty pasta salad: dress hot pasta with the nutty sauce on page 46; cool. This makes a delicious salad and is good made with green and white pasta twists.

Potatoes are one of the cornerstones of cheap and easy cookery. They're economical to buy, quick to prepare and packed with nutrients. And if you add just small quantities of more concentrated foods such as milk, cheese or nuts, they make nourishing main courses.

Baked potatoes are amongst the most popular of all potato dishes, and in this chapter there are ideas for different toppings – from simple butter and grated cheese to spicy hot chilli and tomato.

Many excellent dishes start with raw peeled potatoes, which are then grated and fried to make quick potato crêpes. Or they can be sliced and fried with other tasty ingredients, or sliced and layered in a shallow casserole with cheese and onions then baked in the oven.

Dishes which start with cooked potatoes can be quickly prepared if you have some leftover boiled or mashed potatoes: you can save time by planning for them in advance and cooking extra potato with a previous meal.

baked potatoes

Scrub one or two large potatoes per person, then prick and bake at 220°C/425°F/ Gas 7 for 1–1½ hours, until the potatoes feel soft when squeezed and the skins are crisp. Then split open and serve with butter and grated cheese, or some cottage cheese, soured cream or plain yogurt. Or pour one of the following toppings over the potato halves. Each topping is enough for 4 potatoes.

Mushroom and soured cream: fry 125g/4oz/1½ cups button mushrooms, washed and sliced, in 15g/½oz/1tbsp butter for 2–3 minutes, until just softened, then stir in 150ml/5fl oz/⅔ cup soured cream and salt and pepper to taste. Heat gently – don't boil.

Creamy sweetcorn: put 125g/4oz/heaping ½ cup frozen sweetcorn kernels into a saucepan with 4tbsp cream, mashing the sweetcorn slightly. Stir over the heat until the sweetcorn is hot. Season to taste.

Chilli-tomato-cheese: melt 15g/½oz/1tbsp butter in a medium-sized saucepan and fry 1 small onion, peeled and chopped, for 10 minutes, until soft but not browned. Then add 225g/8oz canned tomatoes, mashing them a bit as you put them in, ½tsp chilli powder and 125g/4oz/ 1 cup grated cheese. Stir gently over the heat until the cheese has melted and the mixture is hot.

stuffed baked potatoes

Serve these with some salad, such as one of the cabbage salads – see pages 73–75, or the crunchy carrot and celery salad on page 76.

see pages 73–75, or the crunchy carrot and celery salad on page 76.

serves 1

Scrub and prick the potatoes, then bake them at 220°C/425°F/Gas 7 for 1–1½ hours until the skins are crisp and the potatoes feel tender inside when squeezed. Halve the potatoes and scoop out the insides. Place the skins on a baking tray. Mash the scooped-out potato with a little butter and milk, half the grated cheese and some salt and pepper. Pile the mixture back into the skins, sprinkle with the remaining grated cheese and put the potatoes back into the oven for about 20 minutes, until golden brown and crisp.

1 or 2 large potatoes
a little butter and milk
25–50g/1–2oz/¼–½ cup grated cheese
seasoning to taste

potato and onion fry

serves 2

1 onion, peeled and sliced	Fry the onion in the oil in a large saucepan for 5 minutes,
2tbsp oil	then add the potatoes and sprinkle with a little salt. Stir,
2 large potatoes, peeled and	then cook over a very gentle heat for 15–20 minutes,
cut into even-sized pieces	until the potatoes are tender and lightly browned, stirring
sea salt	quite often to prevent sticking. Add salt and pepper to
freshly ground black pepper	taste, if necessary, and serve at once.

potatoes with peppers, onions and tomatoes

This is delicious served with a spoonful of soured cream or plain yogurt. Halve these quantities for one serving, using a 225g/8oz can tomatoes.

serves 2–3

1 onion	Peel and slice the onion; deseed and slice the green
1 sweet green pepper	pepper. Fry them in a large saucepan in the oil for
2tbsp oil	5 minutes, then add the potatoes and tomatoes and
2 large potatoes, diced	sprinkle with a little salt. Stir, then cook over a very
400g/14oz can tomatoes	gentle heat for 15–20 minutes, until the potatoes are
sea salt	tender, stirring quite often to prevent sticking. Stir in
2–3tsp mild paprika pepper	the paprika and salt and pepper to taste if necessary.
freshly ground black pepper	Serve at once.

easy potato crêpes

A potato dish which is popular as a children's tea. Halve the ingredients for one serving.

serves 2–4

Grate the potatoes coarsely – there's no need to peel them. Then peel and grate the onion and mix with the potatoes, together with some salt and pepper to taste, the eggs and flour, to make a batter. Heat a little oil in a frying pan and fry tablespoonfuls of the mixture until golden and crispy, turning them over so that both sides are cooked. Drain on paper towels and serve.

2 large potatoes, scrubbed
1 medium-sized onion
sea salt
freshly ground black pepper
2 eggs
3tbsp wholewheat flour
oil for shallow frying

even easier potato crêpe

This is one big crêpe which you cut into wedges and serve as an accompanying dish, or with a salad for a light meal. Or cover the cooked crêpe with sliced tomatoes and grated cheese, grill (broil) or bake until the cheese melts and browns, then serve as an unusual pizza.

serves 2

Grate the potatoes coarsely – there's no need to peel them. Season with salt and pepper. Heat enough oil in a frying pan to cover the base thinly, put in all the potato and press it down to make a flat round shape. Fry until the base is crispy and golden brown, then flip the crêpe over and fry the other side. Drain well and blot with paper towels. Serve at once.

2 large potatoes, scrubbed
sea salt
freshly ground black pepper
oil for shallow frying

cottage pie

This can be prepared in advance, ready for cooking, and only needs a vegetable, such as sprouts or carrots, to go with it. Make a half quantity for two people and bake for 30 minutes, or a quarter of the amount for one person and bake for 15–20 minutes.

serves 4

225g/8oz/heaping 1 cup green lentils
25g/1oz/2tbsp butter
2 large onions, peeled and thinly sliced
1 clove garlic, crushed
1tsp dried mixed herbs
400g/14oz can tomatoes, chopped
2–3tbsp chopped fresh parsley
sea salt
freshly ground black pepper

For the topping
750g/1½lb potatoes, peeled and cut into even-sized pieces
25g/1oz/2tbsp butter
a little milk

To make the lentil base, put the lentils into a large saucepan and cover generously with water. Boil gently until tender, 45–60 minutes. Meanwhile, put the potatoes for the topping into a saucepan, cover with water and boil until just tender when pierced with a knife. Drain both the potatoes and the lentils.

Set the oven to 200°C/400°F/Gas 6. Melt the butter in a large saucepan and fry the onions until tender. Add the garlic, dried mixed herbs, tomatoes, drained lentils and parsley. Season with salt and pepper. Spoon the mixture into a greased shallow ovenproof dish.

Add half the butter and some salt and pepper to the potatoes, then mash the potatoes until smooth, adding a little milk to make a smooth, light consistency. Spoon the potato over the top of the lentil mixture, then spread it out evenly. Run a fork over the top to make ridges, then dot with the remaining butter and bake for 45 minutes, until heated through and golden brown.

potato hotpot

In this tasty family dish the potatoes are parboiled for 10 minutes before layering into the casserole. Halve the quantities for two people, using a 225g/8oz can tomatoes. For one person, it's worth making a half quantity and freezing or keeping what you don't need.

serves 4

Set the oven to 180°C/350°F/Gas 4. Boil the potatoes for 10 minutes, then drain. Arrange layers of potato, onion, tomato and cheese sauce in a greased heatproof dish, seasoning between each layer with basil, pepper and celery salt, and finishing with a layer of potato. Sprinkle with the grated cheese, dot with butter and bake in the oven for 45 minutes. A simply cooked green vegetable goes well with this.

2 large potatoes, peeled and sliced
2 onions, peeled and sliced
400g/14oz can tomatoes
300ml/10fl oz/1¼ cups cheese sauce – see page 12
dried basil
freshly ground black pepper
celery salt
3–4tbsp grated cheese
a little butter

speedy cheesy mash

Incredibly easy and cheap, this is good with some sliced tomato or watercress, or a quickly cooked vegetable. Quarter or halve these quantities for one or two servings.

serves 4

4 large potatoes, peeled and cut into even-sized pieces
25g/1oz/2tbsp butter
2–3tbsp milk
125g/4oz/1 cup grated cheese
sea salt
freshly ground black pepper
1 tomato, thinly sliced

Put the potatoes into a saucepan, cover with cold water and bring to the boil. Boil until the potatoes are tender – about 20 minutes – then drain. Dry the potatoes in the pan over the heat for a minute or two, then mash them with half the butter and add enough milk to make a creamy consistency. Stir in half the grated cheese and season with salt and pepper. Preheat the grill (broiler). Spread the mixture in the grill (broiler) pan, or in a shallow flameproof dish which will fit under the grill (broiler). Sprinkle with the rest of the cheese, arrange the tomato slices on top and dot with the remaining butter. Grill (broil) for about 10 minutes, until golden brown on top and hot inside.

nutty potato cakes

Put the potatoes into a saucepan, cover with cold water and bring to the boil. Boil until potatoes are tender – about 20 minutes – then drain. Dry the potatoes in the pan over the heat for a minute or two, then mash them with the butter and add enough milk to make a creamy consistency. Stir in the chopped nuts and parsley, if available, then season with salt and pepper. Form into potato cakes and coat in wholewheat flour. Pour enough oil into a frying pan to coat the base lightly and set over a moderate heat. When the oil is hot, put in the potato cakes and fry until brown on one side, then turn them over and fry the other side. Serve with a tomato, carrot or cabbage salad, buttered spinach, or grilled (broiled) tomatoes and mushrooms.

4 large potatoes, peeled and cut into even-sized pieces
15g/½oz/1tbsp butter
2–3tbsp milk
125g/4oz/1 cup roughly chopped nuts – any kind, roasted peanuts are cheapest
2 heaped tbsp chopped fresh parsley – if available
sea salt
freshly ground black pepper
plain wholewheat flour for coating
oil for shallow frying

potato and mushroom gratin

Halve the ingredients to make the right amount to serve two people; for one person, either do this and freeze or keep half, or use the following: 1 large potato, 25g/1oz/2tbsp butter, 50g/2oz/ ¾ cup mushrooms, 2 rounded tsp flour and 150ml/5fl oz/ ⅔ cup milk.

serves 4

4 large potatoes, peeled and
cut into even-sized pieces
65g/2½oz/5tbsp butter
175g/6oz/2¼ cups
mushrooms, washed and
sliced
2 rounded tbsp plain
(all-purpose) flour
600ml/1 pint/2½ cups milk
sea salt
freshly ground black pepper
ground mace

Put the potatoes into a saucepan, cover with cold water and bring to the boil. Boil until the potatoes are tender, about 20 minutes.

Meanwhile, melt 50g/2oz/4tbsp of the butter in another saucepan and fry the mushrooms for 2 minutes. Then stir in the flour and milk and stir vigorously over the heat until smooth and thickened; leave to simmer gently for 5–10 minutes, to cook the flour. Season with salt, pepper and a pinch or so of mace.

Preheat the grill (broiler). Drain the potatoes and add them to the mushroom mixture; check the seasoning. Pour the mixture into the grill (broiler) pan or into a shallow flameproof dish which will fit under the grill (broiler). Level the top and dot with the remaining butter. Grill (broil) for about 10 minutes, until golden brown on top and hot inside. A crisp green salad goes well with this, or some cooked peas or carrots.

Vegetables, home-grown, or bought in season, are excellent value for money, as well as being very good for you. They can form the basis of some filling main meals, as well as being indispensable for serving alongside other main courses. Salads, at the end of this chapter, are equally useful, and they, too, can be main courses in their own right as well as being delicious served with other dishes. They are particularly good value, because a few vegetables go a long way when served raw, and of course, they're packed with vitality, too.

green magic

BASIC PREPARATION

The golden rule with vegetables is to trim away as little as possible, then to cook for as short a time as possible in as little water as possible. Stop cooking the vegetables as soon as they're just tender – they're much nicer like this, as well as being more nutritious. This means cooking sprouts for not more than 3–4 minutes, and they're best cut into halves or quarters before cooking. Sliced courgettes (zucchini) take about 2 minutes, cabbage and cauliflower florets about 5 minutes. The exceptions to this rule are root vegetables, which should be just covered with water, but they too, only need to be boiled until they're just tender. Don't let them get anywhere near being soggy.

TO MICROWAVE

All vegetables cook well in the microwave, requiring the minimum of water and retaining their full colour. Prepare the vegetables as usual and cut into even-sized pieces, not too big. Put these into a shallow wide microwave-proof dish so that they are spread out. Sprinkle 2–4tbsp water on top, cover with a plate, then microwave on full until the vegetables are tender, stirring once or twice. After cooking, let the vegetables stand, still covered, for 5–10 minutes, to continue cooking in their own heat. The timing for the vegetables depends on the size of the pieces, the type of vegetable and the quantity being cooked, but as a general rule, potatoes or root vegetables take up to 9 minutes for a 4-serving quantity, about 5 minutes for a single serving; cabbage and spinach take about 6 minutes for 4 servings, 3–4 minutes for 1 serving.

cabbage and cashew nut stir-fry

Quick, easy and delicious. Serve this with some hot boiled rice. The stir-fry can be ready in minutes, but start cooking the brown rice 40–45 minutes before you want to eat the meal – see page 124. For one serving, use 175–225g/6–8oz/3–4 cups prepared cabbage and a quarter of the other ingredients.

serves 4

Wash the cabbage and shred fairly finely, removing any coarse stems. Just before you want to eat, heat the oil in a large saucepan or wok and put in the cabbage and turmeric. Stir-fry for about 3 minutes, until the cabbage has softened a little, then add the coconut, raisins, cashew nuts and some seasoning. Stir well, then serve.

750g/1½lb firm white cabbage, such as Primo or January King
2tbsp oil
1tsp turmeric
2tbsp desiccated (dried shredded) coconut
25–50g/1–2oz/¼–⅓ cup raisins
125g/4oz/1 cup broken cashew nuts
sea salt
freshly ground black pepper

sweet and sour cabbage and peanut stir-fry

A delicious mixture of sweet and sour flavours with the crunch and nourishment of peanuts. If you plan to serve this with brown rice, which goes very well with it, get it on to cook well in advance, as the stir-fry is very quick to make, and the rice takes 40–45 minutes.

serves 2

125g/4oz/scant 1 cup raw peanuts
2tbsp vegetable oil
2 sweet peppers (red and green), deseeded and chopped
1 onion, peeled and chopped
225g/8oz/4 cups cabbage, shredded
2 celery stalks, chopped
2 large carrots, grated

For the dressing
2 cloves garlic, crushed
a walnut-sized piece of fresh ginger, grated
4tbsp soy sauce
4tbsp lemon juice
1tbsp wine vinegar
2tbsp clear honey

First of all make the sweet and sour dressing: put all the ingredients into a small bowl and mix together. Make the stir-fry just before you want to eat – it only takes a few minutes to cook. Fry the peanuts in the oil in a large saucepan or wok for 4–5 minutes, until lightly browned, then add the vegetables and stir-fry for 2 minutes, until they are beginning to soften. Finally pour in the sweet and sour mixture and stir-fry for 1–2 minutes until hot.

ratatouille

This easy-to-make summer stew is good with cooked brown rice or crusty bread and a crisp salad. If you're serving it with brown rice, get this on to cook – see page 124 – before you start the ratatouille, so that they will be ready together. For two servings, halve all the ingredients; for one, use a medium-sized onion, 1 sweet red pepper, 1tbsp olive oil, 1 clove garlic, 1 small courgette (zucchini), 1 small aubergine (eggplant) and 2–3 largish tomatoes.

serves 4

Fry the onions and peppers gently in the oil in a large pan for 5 minutes. Don't let them brown. Then add the garlic, courgettes (zucchini) or marrow (vegetable marrow) and aubergines (eggplants). Stir, then cover the saucepan and cook for 20–25 minutes, until all the vegetables are tender. Then put in the tomatoes and cook, uncovered, for a further 4–5 minutes, to heat the tomatoes through. Season and sprinkle with chopped parsley.

2 large onions, peeled and chopped
450g/1lb sweet red peppers, deseeded and sliced
3tbsp olive oil
3 cloves garlic, crushed
450g/1lb/4 cups courgettes (zucchini) or marrow (vegetable marrow), cut into even-sized pieces
450g/1lb/4 cups aubergines (eggplants), diced
750g/1½lb/3¾ cups tomatoes, peeled and chopped
sea salt
freshly ground black pepper
chopped fresh parsley

la parmigiana

This is quite economical when aubergines (eggplants) are reasonably priced. It's best when made with mozzarella cheese, but any cheese can be used. Serve it with a green salad. Use half these quantities and bake for 30–40 minutes for a two-person quantity; for one person, use 225g/8oz/2 cups diced aubergine (eggplant), a medium-sized onion, 1tbsp oil, 1 small clove garlic, 2 fresh peeled or canned tomatoes, 40–50g/1½–2oz mozzarella cheese and a tablespoonful of Parmesan; bake for about 30 minutes.

serves 4

olive or groundnut (peanut) oil
2 large onions
2 cloves garlic, crushed
1kg/2lb aubergines (eggplants), cut into 1cm/½ inch dice
400g/14oz can tomatoes
225g/8oz cheese, preferably mozzarella, thinly sliced
2–3 heaped tbsp grated Parmesan cheese
sea salt
freshly ground black pepper

Preheat the oven to 200°C/400°F/Gas 6. Heat a little oil in a large saucepan and fry the onions and garlic for about 10 minutes. Remove from the pan with a slotted spoon and fry the aubergine (eggplant) pieces until they're crisp and lightly browned, adding more oil if necessary. Drain and blot the aubergines (eggplants) with paper towels. Layer the aubergines (eggplants), onions, tomatoes and sliced cheese in an ovenproof dish, sprinkling some Parmesan cheese and salt and pepper between the layers and ending with a layer of aubergine (eggplant). Bake, uncovered, in the oven for 40–60 minutes.

root vegetable crumble

Make half these quantities for two people and bake for 20–30 minutes; for one person, make a quarter of the amount and bake in an individual ovenproof dish for 15–20 minutes.

serves 4

Set the oven to 200°C/400°F/Gas 6. Put the vegetables into a shallow ovenproof dish and pour the sauce over them. To make the crumble, put the flour, oats and salt into a bowl and rub in the butter, until there are no pieces visible, then mix in the nuts and grated cheese. Spoon this mixture evenly over the top of the vegetables and sauce, pressing down lightly. Bake for 30–40 minutes, until the top is crisp and lightly browned.

1kg/2lb prepared, cooked root vegetables – carrots, swede (rutabaga), turnips, onions
400ml/14fl oz/1¾ cups béchamel, cheese or mushroom sauce – see page 12, or tomato sauce – see page 13

variations

This crumble topping can be used with any cooked vegetables: cauliflower, courgettes (zucchini), leeks, spinach, or a ratatouille mixture – see page 67. It's also very good with tomatoes and mushrooms: slice and lightly fry 450g/1lb/6 cups button mushrooms, then mix them with 450g/1lb/2½ cups peeled and chopped tomatoes and put the crumble on top.

For the crumble topping
2 heaped tbsp plain wholewheat flour
4 heaped tbsp rolled oats
pinch of salt
50g/2oz/¼ cup butter
50g/2oz/½ cup Brazil nuts or hazelnuts, chopped
50g/2oz/½ cup grated cheese

sweetcorn bake

A simple dish to make, using frozen sweetcorn. Use half these quantities for two people and bake for 20–30 minutes; for one person, use 50g/2oz/heaping ⅓ cup sweetcorn, 5tbsp milk and 1 egg. Serve with some sliced tomatoes and crusty bread.

serves 4

25g/1oz/2tbsp butter
300ml/10fl oz/1¼ cups milk
4 slices of wholewheat bread, crusts removed
225g/8oz/heaping 1 cup frozen sweetcorn kernels, thawed in a sieve (strainer) under hot running water
2 eggs
pinch of cayenne pepper or chilli powder – optional
sea salt
freshly ground black pepper
50g/2oz/½ cup grated cheese

Preheat the oven to 190°C/375°F/Gas 5. Heat the butter and milk in a saucepan until the butter has melted, remove from the heat and crumble in the bread. Set aside while you grease a shallow ovenproof dish, then mix the bread and milk, breaking up any large pieces, and beat in the rest of the ingredients except for the cheese. Pour the mixture into the dish, sprinkle with the cheese and bake for 35–40 minutes, until set and golden brown.

cauliflower and green pea terrine

This is a stripy terrine for serving cold with some salad and crusty bread.

serves 4

Set the oven to 170°C/325°F/Gas 3. Line a 450g/1lb loaf pan (measuring about 18 x 10 x 7.5cm/6 x 4 x 3 inches) with a long strip of greaseproof (waxed) or non-stick paper to cover the bottom and narrow sides; grease well. Melt the butter in a saucepan and stir in the flour; cook for a few seconds until the flour froths, then add the milk. Stir well, over the heat, until the mixture thickens. Let it simmer gently for 10 minutes, then remove from the heat and beat in the egg. Whizz half the sauce with the cauliflower and cheese in the food processor or blender; season. Transfer to a bowl. Whizz the rest of the sauce with the peas and mint in the food processor or blender; season. Put half the green pea mixture into the base of the loaf pan, level; spoon half the cauliflower mixture on top, then put in the rest of the pea mixture, and finally the rest of the cauliflower mixture. Stand the loaf pan in a roasting pan, half fill the roasting pan with boiling water and bake for 1 hour, or until the terrine is firm. Leave to get completely cold, then chill. Loosen the sides of the terrine, turn it out, and serve in slices.

40g/1½oz/3tbsp butter
1 heaped and 1 level tbsp plain (all-purpose) flour
300ml/10fl oz/1¼ cups milk
1 egg
½ small cauliflower, cooked and drained
50g/2oz/½ cup grated cheese
sea salt
freshly ground black pepper
125g/4oz/1 cup frozen peas
1tbsp chopped fresh mint

broccoli roulade with mushroom filling

serves 3-4

450g/1lb fresh trimmed or frozen broccoli
15g/½oz/1tbsp butter
sea salt
freshly ground black pepper
4 eggs, separated
a little grated Parmesan cheese

For the filling
15g/½oz/1tbsp butter
175g/6oz/2¼ cups button mushrooms, washed and sliced
1tsp cornflour (cornstarch)
150ml/5fl oz/⅔ cup single (light) cream
grated nutmeg

Cook the fresh broccoli in 1cm/½ inch boiling water for 6–7 minutes, until tender; drain well. Cook frozen broccoli according to package instructions; drain well. Whizz the broccoli in the food processor or blender, then add the butter, a little salt and pepper and the egg yolks.

Line a shallow Swiss roll tin (jelly roll pan) measuring 18 x 27.5cm/7 x 11 inches with greased greaseproof (waxed) paper to cover the base and extend 5cm/2 inches up each side. Sprinkle with Parmesan cheese. Set the oven to 200°C/400°F/Gas 6. Whisk the egg whites until stiff but not dry and fold them into the broccoli mixture. Pour into the prepared tin (pan) and bake for 10–15 minutes, until risen and springy to the touch.

Meanwhile, make the filling. Heat the butter in a saucepan and fry the mushrooms for 2–3 minutes. Add the cornflour (cornstarch) and cream and stir until thickened. Add salt, pepper and grated nutmeg.

Have ready a large piece of greaseproof (waxed) paper dusted with Parmesàn cheese and turn the roulade out on to this; strip off the paper from the roulade. Spread the filling over the roulade, roll it up and slide it on to an ovenproof serving dish. Heat through in the oven for 5 minutes. Serve immediately.

cabbage-based salads

Firm white or pale green cabbages are available all year round, are always good value, and make an excellent salad base. Wash the cabbage, opening between the layers as well as you can, to remove traces of any chemicals. Then grate the cabbage, or shred it finely with a knife, and leave it in fine shreds, or chop these up into small pieces. If you have a food processor, you can put the cabbage into this in chunks, along with any other ingredients which need chopping, such as carrot and onion. Add some dressing and your salad is ready in moments.

crunchy cabbage and peanut salad

For a main-meal salad for one person, make half this quantity.

serves 2–4

Finely shred the cabbage. Scrape and coarsely grate the carrots. Deseed and chop the red pepper. Put all these vegetables into a bowl and add enough vinaigrette to moisten them and make them shiny. Then add the other ingredients and mix well. If you don't intend to serve the salad immediately, save the peanuts to add at the last minute, so that they stay crunchy.

350g/12oz white cabbage
2 large carrots
1 sweet red pepper
vinaigrette dressing – see page 80
2tbsp chopped fresh parsley, chives or spring (green) onions
2tbsp raisins
50g/2oz/scant ½ cup roasted peanuts

crunchy cabbage and apple salad

Make half this quantity for a main-meal salad for one; if there's some over, it will keep in the fridge for a day.

serves 2–4

450g/1lb/8 cups white
cabbage, finely shredded
2 apples, cored and diced
2 cooked beetroots (beets),
peeled and diced
2 celery stalks, chopped
6 spring (green) onions,
sliced
vinaigrette dressing – see
page 80 – to moisten

Put all the salad ingredients into a bowl and mix together.

coleslaw

Make a third of this quantity for one person, using a small onion and a smallish carrot.

Put the cabbage, carrot, onions and raisins or sultanas (golden raisins), if you're using them, into a large bowl. Add your chosen dressing and stir in, to make a creamy mixture. Season.

450g/1lb/8 cups white cabbage, finely shredded
225g/8oz/1⅓ cups carrots, scraped and coarsely grated
2 onions, peeled and finely chopped
3–4tbsp raisins or sultanas (golden raisins) – optional
3–4tbsp good-quality mayonnaise, mixed half and half with plain yogurt; or just plain yogurt; or soured cream blended with
1tsp made mustard
sea salt
freshly ground black pepper

root-based salads

Root vegetables – carrots, swede (rutabaga), celeriac (celery root) and raw beetroot (beet) – make good substantial salads. Like cabbage salad, these can make a filling light meal on their own or with some bread or a baked potato. To grate the vegetables, use the coarse side of a box grater which you can stand on a board or over a bowl, or use the grating attachment on the food processor if you have one.

crunchy carrot and celery salad

This goes well as an accompaniment to a soft-textured main course such as a soufflé. Halve the quantities for a main meal for one, quarter them for an accompaniment.

serves 2–4

3–4 carrots
1 good-sized celery heart
1 small sweet green pepper
vinaigrette dressing –
see page 80
sea salt
freshly ground black pepper

Coarsely grate the carrots. Chop the celery. Deseed and chop the green pepper. Put the vegetables into a bowl and moisten with dressing. Mix well until everything is coated with the dressing. Adjust the seasoning if necessary.

variation

Use 1 large or 2 smaller fennel bulbs instead of the celery, and a bunch of spring (green) onions, finely chopped, instead of the green pepper.

rémoulade

If using mayonnaise or yogurt for the dressing, stir in a little Dijon mustard if you like.

serves 4

Peel the celeriac (celery root) and grate it coarsely or cut it into fine matchsticks. Put it into a bowl and add enough of your chosen dressing to moisten. Season.

450g/1lb celeriac (celery root)
vinaigrette dressing – see page 80; or good-quality mayonnaise; or mayonnaise and plain yogurt
sea salt
freshly ground black pepper

raw beetroot salad

serves 4

Peel and coarsely grate the beetroots (beets). Put them into a bowl with the apple, and the raisins if you're using them. Add enough vinaigrette to moisten. Season.

450g/1lb raw beetroots (beets)
1 apple, grated
4tbsp raisins – optional
vinaigrette dressing – see page 80
sea salt
freshly ground black pepper

tomato-based salads

There's no salad nicer than one made from firm, juicy tomatoes, and when they're in season it can be made quite economically. Tomato salad goes well with many savoury dishes, adding just the right touch of moisture as well as a flash of vivid colour. Or, if you add some little cubes of cheese to a tomato salad, it can become a meal in itself – lovely with some crusty French bread.

Tomato and onion salad: allow a large tomato and a few raw onion rings for each person. Wash the tomato and slice it thinly: the tomatoes don't need peeling if they're good and firm, as they should be for this salad. Put the tomato and onion into a shallow dish, sprinkle with a little sea salt and freshly ground black pepper and a few drops of olive oil. You can add a few drops of wine vinegar just before serving, if you like, but don't put it on too soon, or the tomato juices will run too much. Some torn fresh basil is the perfect finishing touch.

Greek salad: for this delicious, substantial salad, for each person you need: 1–2 large tomatoes, a 5cm/2 inch piece of cucumber, a few slices of raw onion, 3 or 4 large juicy black olives, 25–50g/1–2oz feta cheese and a little vinaigrette. Slice the tomatoes; peel and dice the cucumber. Mix these in a bowl with the onion, olives, cubed cheese and enough vinaigrette just to moisten. Serve with crusty bread.

Tomato, cucumber and celery salad: wash and slice 1 bunch of celery. Slice 4 firm tomatoes. Peel and slice ½ cucumber. Put all the ingredients into a bowl, add some lemon juice or vinaigrette, salt and freshly ground black pepper and mix together.

green-based salads

Green salad is useful for serving with many cooked dishes, particularly many of the quick dishes in this book. It is helpful for the cook in a hurry, because it's much quicker than cooking vegetables. You do need crisp, fresh ingredients: crisp lettuce and/or watercress as a base, to which other ingredients can be added as available – some tender spinach leaves are nice shredded into it, so are a few dandelion leaves or some rocket (arugula), which has a hot, spicy flavour. Fresh herbs can be added as available, and onion or spring (green) onion can be added to taste.

green salad

serves 2–3

Tear the lettuce into bite-sized pieces and put into a bowl with any herbs you may have. Just before serving the salad, spoon a little vinaigrette on to it and turn the salad until the leaves are all coated. Serve immediately.

1 lettuce, washed and dried in a salad spinner or by patting lightly with a clean cloth
chopped fresh herbs – as available
vinaigrette dressing – see page 80

vinaigrette dressing

A quick-to-make and useful basic for all salads. If you make plenty in a jar, it will keep well in the fridge for several days, ready for when you need it. These quantities can be multiplied up.

1 clove garlic, crushed
1tsp salt
1tbsp made mustard
3tbsp red wine vinegar
10tbsp best-quality olive oil
freshly ground black pepper

Put all the ingredients into a screwtop jar and shake vigorously until blended and quite thick looking. Check the flavouring: more crushed garlic can be added, or more salt.

Packing vegetables with a tasty stuffing is a great way to make a few ingredients go a long way and provide a tasty meal, or even one that's a bit special. The stuffing can be made from a cooked rice, breadcrumb, potato or other vegetable base; or it can be made from other tasty vegetables such as mushrooms, mixed with more concentrated protein-providing ingredients such as chopped nuts or grated cheese. For extra appeal and nourishment, the vegetables can be served with a well-flavoured sauce.

great stuff

stuffed peppers

This is a light and tasty, but filling, stuffing for peppers and one which can be varied according to vegetables in season. The mushrooms can be replaced by the same quantity of finely diced courgettes (zucchini) or by a 400g/14oz can chick peas (garbanzo beans), drained. They're good served with a tomato or cheese sauce. For two people, just halve the ingredients, and for one person, just quarter them, using a small onion and 2tsp oil.

serves 4

4 sweet green peppers

For the filling
1 large onion, peeled and finely chopped
2tbsp oil
225g/8oz/3 cups mushrooms, washed and chopped
125g/4oz/1 cup mixed nuts, finely chopped or ground in the food processor
125g/4oz/heaping ½ cup tomatoes, peeled and chopped
1tsp mixed dried herbs
1–2tsp yeast extract
sea salt
freshly ground black pepper
4 heaped tbsp grated cheese

Cut the tops off the green peppers and reserve. Scoop out the seeds and discard. Wash the peppers, then boil them in water for 5 minutes, until they are beginning to get tender. Drain them thoroughly, then pat them dry on paper towels. Stand them upright in a greased ovenproof dish.

Set the oven to 180°C/350°F/Gas 4. Fry the onion in the oil for 10 minutes, until tender, then add the mushrooms and cook for a further 2–3 minutes. Remove from the heat and stir in the nuts, tomatoes, herbs, yeast extract and salt and pepper to taste. Spoon this mixture into the peppers, then sprinkle with grated cheese and replace the cut-off tops. Bake for 25–30 minutes.

stuffed avocado

A hot stuffed avocado makes an easy and luxurious meal and can be quite economical when avocados are reasonably priced. Serve on a base of cooked rice or creamy mashed potato. Make sure the avocado is really ripe: it should feel slightly soft all over, like a dessert pear does when it's just right for eating. For one person, choose a small avocado and halve the stuffing ingredients.

serves 2

Set the oven to 200°C/400°F/Gas 6. Cut the avocado in half, twist the halves in opposite directions and pull apart, then remove the stone. Brush the cut flesh of the avocado with lemon juice. Put the avocado halves into a shallow ovenproof dish. Fry the onion and green pepper in the butter for 10 minutes, then remove from the heat and add the tomato, garlic, parsley, Tabasco and salt and pepper to taste. Spoon this mixture into the middle of the avocados, sprinkle the grated cheese on top and bake them for 20 minutes, until just heated through. Be careful not to leave them too long, as avocado gets a funny flavour if it's overcooked.

1 large ripe avocado
lemon juice
1 onion, peeled and chopped
½ sweet green pepper, deseeded and finely chopped
15g/½oz/1tbsp butter
1 tomato, peeled and chopped
1 clove garlic, crushed
1tbsp chopped fresh parsley
1–2 drops of Tabasco
sea salt
freshly ground black pepper
2tbsp grated cheese

aubergines provençales

These make a meal that's a bit special and they're well worth the trouble because they work out quite economical when aubergines (eggplants) are reasonably priced. Although I don't usually salt aubergines (eggplants) before cooking these days, in this recipe it softens the flesh, which helps with the cooking later. Serve with sautéed or new potatoes or creamy mashed potato, and a lightly cooked green vegetable. For one person, halve these quantities, using a small onion.

serves 2

1 large aubergine (eggplant) or 2 smaller ones, about 450g/1lb altogether
sea salt
olive or groundnut (peanut) oil
1 large onion, peeled and chopped
2 tomatoes, peeled and chopped
1–2 cloves garlic, crushed
1tbsp chopped fresh parsley
freshly ground black pepper

For the topping
2tbsp soft wholewheat breadcrumbs
a little butter

Remove the stem and cut the aubergine (eggplant) in half lengthways. Make lots of cuts across the flesh without piercing the skin and sprinkle with salt, putting it in between the cuts. Leave for 30 minutes. Then rinse the aubergine (eggplant) halves under cold water and squeeze as much liquid out of them as you can. Scoop the flesh out of the skins and chop the flesh.

Set the oven to 200°C/400°F/Gas 6. Heat a little oil in a large saucepan and fry the skins for about 3 minutes on both sides. Remove from the pan and place in a shallow ovenproof dish. Then fry the onion and the aubergine (eggplant) flesh for 7 minutes. Add the tomatoes and garlic and fry for a further 3 minutes. Add the parsley and season with salt and pepper. Spoon this mixture into the skins, sprinkle with the crumbs and dot with butter. Bake for 20–30 minutes.

stuffed cabbage rolls

These are a bit fiddly to make, but a great way of creating a filling and interesting meal out of practically nothing. Serve with baked potatoes and another cooked vegetable, such as carrots, or a crunchy carrot and celery salad – see page 76. The quantities can easily be quartered or halved if you're making this for one or two people; in this case, reduce the cooking time to 20–30 minutes.

serves 4

Set the oven to 190°C/375°F/Gas 5. Put the cabbage leaves into a saucepan of boiling water for 2–3 minutes, to soften them, then drain well. Fry the onion in the oil for 10 minutes, then add the nuts, breadcrumbs, tomatoes and seasoning. Divide the mixture between the cabbage leaves, roll them up and place them side by side in a greased shallow ovenproof dish. Pour the sauce over the cabbage rolls, sprinkle with the grated cheese and bake for 40–45 minutes, until golden brown and bubbling.

8 outer leaves of cabbage –
Savoy, Primo or January
King
1 onion, peeled and chopped
2tbsp oil
125g/4oz/1 cup walnuts or
roasted peanuts, chopped
12 heaped tbsp soft
wholewheat breadcrumbs
400g/14oz can tomatoes
sea salt
freshly ground black pepper
300ml/10fl oz/1¼ cups
cheese sauce – see page 12
50g/2oz/½ cup grated
cheese

tomatoes with spicy stuffing

Those big tomatoes – beefsteak tomatoes – make a filling meal when stuffed with this spicy potato mixture and served with some cooked rice and a green salad. Halve these ingredients for one person.

serves 2

2 large beefsteak tomatoes
sea salt
1 onion, peeled and chopped
2tbsp oil
225g/8oz/1¾ cups potato, peeled and cut into 6mm/¼ inch dice
1 clove garlic, crushed
1tsp cumin seeds
½tsp turmeric
freshly ground black pepper

Cut the tops off the tomatoes, then scoop out the pulp. Chop the pulp and spread it evenly over the base of a lightly greased shallow ovenproof dish that's big enough to hold the two tomatoes. Sprinkle the inside of each tomato with salt, then turn them upside down to drain. Next, make the potato filling. Fry the onion in the oil for 5 minutes, then add the potato and garlic. Cook gently for 10 minutes, then add the spices and cook for another 4–5 minutes, until all the potato is just tender. Season.

Set the oven to 200°C/400°F/Gas 6. Spoon the potato mixture into the tomatoes. Stand the tomatoes in the dish on top of the tomato pulp and replace their tops. Bake for 15–20 minutes, until the tomatoes are just tender.

easy as pie

Being able to make good pastry is one of the most useful assets for the busy, budget-conscious cook. It enables you to turn a few bits and pieces into a good meal, at very little expense, and is universally popular and appealing.

You can use all wholewheat flour for making pastry if you like, but these days I use a half-and-half mixture of wholewheat and white flour for all my pastry. It's light and very tasty.

One tip: when you're handling any kind of wholewheat pastry, it helps to roll the pastry out on a board, then you can tip it straight from the board into your pan or dish, avoiding any breakages.

quick quiche

This is a quick quiche made with a very light pastry which melts in your mouth and doesn't need to be baked blind. If you're cooking for one, this mixture is delicious made into individual-sized quiches using deepish old saucers or 10cm/4 inch quiche pans or glass dishes. Use half these ingredients to make one quiche, or make two and freeze or keep one for later. Bake these quiches for about 20 minutes.

serves 2–4 as a main meal

For the pastry
125g/4oz/¾ cup + 2tbsp self-raising wholewheat flour or a half-and-half mix of white and wholewheat self-raising flour
½tsp salt
65g/2½oz/5tbsp butter

For the filling
150ml/5fl oz/⅔ cup milk – or single (light) cream for a luxury version
2 eggs
2tbsp finely chopped onion
2 heaped tbsp chopped fresh parsley
sea salt
freshly ground black pepper

Set the oven to 190°C/375°F/Gas 5. Put a baking sheet into the middle of the oven to heat up. Lightly grease a 20cm/8 inch quiche pan.

Put the flour into a bowl with the salt and rub in the butter with your fingertips until the mixture looks like fine breadcrumbs. Press the mixture together to make a dough – as the proportion of butter is a little higher than usual, you shouldn't need any water. Roll out the pastry and ease into the pan; press down and trim the edges.

Whisk together the milk or cream and the eggs. Add the onion and parsley, and seasoning to taste. Pour the mixture into the quiche case and place in the oven on the baking sheet. Bake for 35–40 minutes, until the filling is set and lightly browned. Serve hot or warm.

variations

Carrot quiche: use 1 large grated carrot instead of, or as well as, the parsley.

Mushroom quiche: use 125g/4oz/1 cup button mushrooms, thinly sliced. Omit or keep the parsley, whichever you prefer.

Spring (green) onion quiche: omit the onion and parsley and use 1 bunch of spring (green) onions, finely chopped, instead.

Sweetcorn quiche: use 125g/4oz/heaping ½ cup frozen sweetcorn kernels instead of the onion and parsley.

Cheese and tomato quiche: omit the parsley and use 50–125g/2–4oz/½–1 cup grated cheese and 1 tomato, thinly sliced.

Mint and pea quiche: use 2tbsp finely chopped fresh mint instead of the parsley, and 125g/4oz/scant 1 cup frozen peas. This is good with or without the onion.

Quick beany quiche: add ½tsp made mustard to the eggs and milk and put the well-drained contents of half a 400g/14oz can butter or lima beans, chick peas (garbanzo beans) or cannellini beans on the pastry before pouring in the milk mixture. If you prefer, leave out the onion and parsley. A crushed clove of garlic mixed in with the eggs is also nice in this, and so are a few juicy black olives, depending on how flavourful you like your quiches.

more quick quiches

In these recipes, the pastry case is baked in the oven while you're preparing the filling.

basic pastry quiche case

This recipe makes the quiche case for the recipes on the following three pages. Divide quantities in half to make one smaller quiche for one person, using an old, deep saucer or a 10cm/4 inch quiche pan or dish, and baking for 10 minutes.

makes one 20cm/8 inch quiche case or two 10cm/4 inch quiche cases

125g/4oz/¾ cup + 2tbsp plain wholewheat flour or a half-and-half mix of plain white (all-purpose) flour and wholewheat flour
pinch of salt
50g/2oz/¼ cup butter
6tsp cold water

Set the oven to 200°C/400°F/Gas 6. Put a baking sheet into the middle of the oven to heat up. Lightly grease a 20cm/8 inch quiche pan.

Sift the flour into a large bowl, adding any residue of bran from the sieve (strainer). Add the salt, then rub in the butter until the mixture looks like fine breadcrumbs. Mix to a dough with the water. Roll out the pastry and ease it into the pan; press down and trim the edges. Put the quiche into the oven to bake for 10 minutes while you're preparing the filling.

poverty pie

A friend gave me this recipe for what in her family is referred to as 'poverty pie' – an end of the week dish to put together from storecupboard ingredients and oddments from the fridge. To make the pie for one person, halve all the ingredients except for the egg, and bake for 15–20 minutes.

serves 4

Set the oven to 200°C/400°F/Gas 6. Bake the quiche case for 10 minutes, as described in the previous recipe.

While the quiche case is cooking, make the filling. Put the butter, flour and milk into a saucepan and whisk over a moderate heat until thickened. Remove from the heat and add most of the cheese, the egg yolk and mustard, and salt and pepper to taste. Whisk the egg white until stiff, then fold it into the mixture.

Pour the mixture into the quiche case, sprinkle with the rest of the cheese and put into the oven. Turn the heat down to 190°C/375°F/Gas 5. Bake for 20 minutes, until puffed up and golden brown.

1 basic pastry quiche case – see previous recipe

For the filling
25g/1oz/2tbsp butter
1 rounded tbsp plain (all-purpose) flour
300ml/10fl oz/1½ cups milk
50–125g/2–4oz/½–1 cup grated cheese
1 egg, separated
½tsp made mustard
sea salt
freshly ground black pepper

mixed vegetable quiche

You can use leftover cooked vegetables for this, or the mixture of cauliflower and frozen mixed vegetables given in the recipe.

serves 4
as a main course

1 basic pastry quiche case – see page 90

For the filling
1 small cauliflower or ½ larger one, washed and broken into even-sized small florets – cut larger ones if necessary
300g/10oz/2 cups frozen mixed vegetables
300ml/10fl oz/1¼ cups cheese sauce – see page 12
sea salt
freshly ground black pepper
2tbsp grated cheese

Set the oven to 200°C/400°F/Gas 6. Bake the quiche case for 10 minutes, as described on page 90.

While the quiche case is cooking, make the filling. Pour 1cm/½ inch water into a medium-sized saucepan and bring up to the boil, then add the cauliflower and mixed vegetables and boil for 4–5 minutes, until the cauliflower is just tender. Drain well. Add these vegetables to the cheese sauce; season.

Spoon the mixture into the quiche case and sprinkle with the grated cheese. Pop the quiche back into the oven for 15 minutes or so, just to brown the top. Serve hot.

sweetcorn soufflé quiche

A quick and easy quiche which is a bit different. The filling rises and there is quite a generous amount, so if you're cooking for one or two people, use this quantity of pastry to make two 10cm/4 inch quiche cases, then use 1 egg and halve all the other filling ingredients. Bake for about 15 minutes.

serves 4

Set the oven to 200°C/400°F/Gas 6. Bake the quiche case for 10 minutes, as described on page 90.

While the quiche case is cooking, make the filling. Put the butter, flour and milk into a saucepan and whisk over a moderate heat until thickened. Remove from the heat and add the sweetcorn, most of the cheese, the egg yolk, mustard, and salt and pepper to taste. Whisk the egg white until stiff, then fold it into the mixture.

Pour the mixture into the quiche case, sprinkle with the rest of the cheese and put into the oven. Turn the heat down to 190°C/375°F/Gas 5. Bake for 30 minutes, until puffed up and golden brown.

1 basic pastry quiche case – see page 90

For the filling
25g/1oz/2tbsp butter
1 rounded tbsp plain (all-purpose) flour
300ml/10fl oz/1¼ cups milk
125g/4oz/heaping ½ cup frozen sweetcorn kernels
50–125g/2–4oz/½–1 cup grated cheese
1 egg, separated
½tsp made mustard
sea salt
freshly ground black pepper

mushroom quiche

This quiche is a good one to make when mushrooms are cheap, or if you have some field mushrooms. These quantities make a lovely big shallow quiche, using a pan measuring 30cm/12 inches across; alternatively, you could use two 20cm/8 inch pans, or halve the ingredients if you prefer. For two people, halve the ingredients and use a 20cm/8 inch quiche pan; for one person, use a quarter of the quantities (2–3tbsp soured cream) and a 10cm/4 inch quiche pan.

serves 6
as a main course

a double quantity of pastry
– see basic pastry quiche
case on page 90

For the filling
1 onion, peeled and chopped
25g/1oz/2tbsp butter
450g/1lb/6 cups button
mushrooms, washed and
sliced
1–2 cloves garlic, crushed
1tsp cornflour (cornstarch)
150ml/5fl oz/⅔ cup soured
cream
sea salt
freshly ground black pepper
grated nutmeg
chopped fresh parsley

Set the oven to 200°C/400°F/Gas 6. Put a baking sheet into the middle of the oven to heat up. Lightly grease a 30cm/12 inch quiche pan. Roll out the pastry and ease it into the pan; press down and trim the edges. Put the quiche into the oven to bake for 10–15 minutes while you're preparing the filling.

To make the filling, fry the onion in the butter for 10 minutes, then add the mushrooms and garlic and cook for a further 3–4 minutes. Stir in the cornflour (cornstarch) and the soured cream; cook for a moment or two until thickened. Then remove from the heat and season with salt, pepper and nutmeg.

Spoon the mushroom filling into the quiche case; return the quiche to the oven for 10–15 minutes to heat through. Serve hot, sprinkled with parsley.

potato and mushroom pasties

These quantities can easily be quartered or halved for one or two people.

makes 4

First make the filling. Fry the onion in the oil for 5 minutes, then add the potato, garlic and mushrooms. Cook gently for 10 minutes or until the vegetables are just tender and any liquid produced by the mushrooms has disappeared. Season with salt and pepper. Leave to cool.

Set the oven to 200°C/400°F/Gas 6. Make the pastry as described in the basic pastry quiche case on page 90 and divide it into 4 pieces; roll each piece into a circle 15cm/6 inches across. Spoon a quarter of the potato mixture on to each, fold up the pastry into a pasty shape and press the edges together. Make a couple of small steam holes in each pasty, then place the pasties on a baking tray and bake for 20–25 minutes.

225g/8oz/1½ cups plain wholewheat flour or a half-and-half mix of plain white (all-purpose) flour and wholewheat flour
½tsp salt
125g/4oz/½ cup butter
3tbsp water

For the filling
1 onion, peeled and chopped
2tbsp oil
225g/8oz/heaping 1½ cups potato, peeled and cut into 6mm/¼ inch dice
1 clove garlic, crushed
225g/8oz/3 cups mush-rooms, washed and chopped
sea salt
freshly ground black pepper

cheese and onion pie

This is a basic recipe, followed by three variations. Divide quantities in half to make one smaller pie for two people, or use a quarter of these quantities for one person, using an old, deep saucer or a small ovenproof dish, and baking for 20 minutes.

serves 4

225g/8oz/1½ cups plain wholewheat flour or a half-and-half mix of plain white (all-purpose) flour and wholewheat flour
pinch of salt
125g/4oz/½ cup butter
3tbsp cold water

For the filling
3 large onions, sliced
sea salt
175g/6oz/1½ cups grated cheese
freshly ground black pepper
grated nutmeg

Sift the flour into a large bowl, adding any residue of bran from the sieve (strainer). Add the salt, then rub in the butter until the mixture looks like fine breadcrumbs. Mix to a dough with the water. Set aside to chill while you prepare the filling.

Cook the onions in 2.5cm/1 inch boiling salted water for 5 minutes, to soften slightly. Drain and cool.

Set the oven to 220°C/425°F/Gas 7. Put a baking sheet into the middle of the oven to heat up. Roll out half the pastry to fit a 20–22.5cm/8–9 inch pie plate. Mix the cheese with the onions and seasonings to taste. Spoon the onion mixture on top of the pastry. Roll out the remaining pastry to fit the top; press the edges together and trim. Bake for 30 minutes.

variations

Butter bean, cheese and pickle pie: make this in the same way as cheese and onion pie, using 125g/4oz/ heaping ½ cup butter or lima beans, soaked, cooked and drained, or a 400g/14oz can, drained, in place of one of the onions, and reducing the amount of cheese to 50g/2oz/½ cup. Add 2 heaped tbsp pickle or chutney to the mixture before spooning on the pastry.

Cabbage pie: this is very good with a sauce made by mixing some chopped fresh herbs into a small carton of soured cream or plain yogurt.

Fry a chopped onion and 450g/1lb/8 cups shredded white cabbage in 25g/1oz/2tbsp butter until they are tender – 10 minutes. Add 3–4tbsp chopped fresh parsley, 75–125g/3 4oz/¾–1 cup chopped button mushrooms, 2 peeled and chopped tomatoes, 1tsp dried dillweed or caraway seeds, and salt and pepper to taste. Assemble and cook the pie as described in cheese and onion pie.

Root vegetable pie with cheesy pastry: add 125g/4oz/ 1 cup grated cheese to the pastry after you have rubbed in the butter and before you add the water. To make the filling, fry a chopped onion and 2 chopped celery stalks in 25g/1oz/2tbsp butter for 10 minutes, then add 225g/8oz/1½ cups chopped carrots, 225g/8oz/1½ cups each peeled and diced swede (rutabaga) and turnips or parsnips and 150ml/5fl oz/⅔ cup water. Cover and cook gently for about 15 minutes, until the vegetables are just tender. Season and cool. Assemble and cook the pie as described in cheese and onion pie.

steamed vegetable pudding

Other combinations of vegetables can be used for this, depending on what's available. A half quantity can be made in a small bowl and steamed for 1 hour, for two people; or a quarter quantity can be made in a deepish ramekin or an old cup for one person, using 50g/2oz/6tbsp flour, 25g/1oz/2tbsp butter and 2–3tsp water for the pastry and a quarter of the filling ingredients. Steam this for 45 minutes.

serves 4

175g/6oz/1 cup + 3tbsp self-raising wholewheat flour or a half-and-half mix of white and wholewheat self-raising flour
½tsp salt
75g/3oz/6tbsp butter
2–3tbsp water

For the filling
1 onion, peeled and chopped
2 potatoes, peeled and cut into 1cm/½ inch dice
2 carrots, scraped and sliced
225g/8oz/3 cups mushrooms, sliced
2tbsp soy sauce
sea salt
freshly ground black pepper

Parboil the vegetables, except the mushrooms, for 10 minutes; drain. Grease a 900ml/1½ pint/3¾ cup pudding bowl well with butter. Put the flour into a bowl with the salt, then add the butter and rub it in with your fingertips. Add enough water to make a dough. Turn this out on to a floured board and knead lightly, then roll out two-thirds to fit the bowl; press down well. Put in the vegetables, mushrooms, soy sauce and seasoning. Roll out the other piece of dough to fit the top of the pudding and press down firmly; trim the edges. Prick the top several times with a fork, then cover with a piece of greaseproof (waxed) paper and a piece of foil and tie down. Stand the bowl in a large saucepan with enough water to come halfway up the sides of the bowl, and simmer gently for 1½ hours. Keep the water level topped up with boiling water while the pudding is steaming.

To serve, remove the coverings, slip a palette knife (metal spatula) around the sides of the bowl to loosen the pudding, then turn it out on to a warmed plate. Serve with lightly cooked vegetables or a salad.

quick pizza

serves 4–6

Set the oven to 220°C/425°F/Gas 7. Put the flour, mustard powder, baking powder and ½tsp salt into a bowl, then add the butter and rub it in with your fingertips. Add the milk mixture and the grated cheese and mix to a soft but not sticky dough. Turn out on to a floured board and knead lightly, then roll out to fit a large baking sheet or round pizza dish. Prick the dough all over. Pop this into the oven for 10 minutes while you prepare the topping. To do this, first fry the onions in the oil for 10 minutes, then add the tomato paste and salt and pepper to taste. Spread this over the pizza base, then put the mushrooms and green pepper on top. Sprinkle with the grated cheese and oregano. Put the pizza back into the oven and bake for 20–25 minutes, until puffed up and golden brown on top. A crisp green salad goes well with this.

225g/8oz/1½ cups self-raising wholewheat flour or a half-and-half mix of white and wholewheat self-raising flour
½tsp mustard powder
2tsp baking powder
sea salt
50g/2oz/¼ cup butter
150ml/5fl oz/⅔ cup milk and water mixed
40g/1½oz/5tbsp grated cheese

For the topping
2 onions, peeled and chopped
2tbsp oil
2tbsp tomato paste
freshly ground black pepper
50g/2oz/¾ cup button mushrooms, sliced
1 small sweet green pepper, deseeded and sliced
50g/2oz/½ cup grated cheese
2tsp dried oregano

yeast pizza

serves 4–6

450g/1lb/3 cups plain
wholewheat flour or
a half-and-half mix of plain
white (all-purpose) flour
and wholewheat flour
1 sachet (package) of easy-
blend (rapid-rise) dried yeast
sea salt
about 175ml/6fl oz/¾ cup
warm water
2tbsp oil

For the topping
2 large onions, peeled and
chopped
oil
4tbsp tomato paste
1 clove garlic, crushed
freshly ground black pepper
125g/4oz/1½ cups
mushrooms, washed and
sliced, or 1 sweet green
pepper, deseeded and sliced
125g/4oz sliced cheese –
preferably mozzarella
a few black olives – optional
dried oregano

Make the dough. Put the flours, yeast, ½tsp salt, water and oil into a bowl and mix to a dough. Turn the dough out on to a lightly floured work surface and continue to knead, stretch and pummel it with your hands for 5 minutes. You will find that it becomes smooth and silky. Put the dough into a bowl, cover with a damp cloth and leave until the dough has doubled in size. This takes about 1 hour in a warm place, or up to 3 hours at room temperature. Then punch down the dough, divide it between two well-greased quiche pans or one larger one, or press it into a large round shape on a baking tray. Put it in a warm place while you make the filling.

Fry the onions in 2tbsp oil for 10 minutes, then add the tomato paste, garlic and salt and pepper to taste. Set the oven to 250°C/500°F/Gas 9.

Flatten the dough with your hands, pressing it well into the pans and up the sides a little. Spread the tomato mixture on top of the dough, then put the mushrooms or green pepper, cheese and olives on top. Drizzle a little oil over the top and sprinkle with oregano. Bake the pizzas for 15–20 minutes, until puffed up and golden brown on top.

Nuts feature in recipes in a number of other sections of this book. They are a useful food, because although they sound expensive – and are if used in large quantities – a little goes a long way, and a dish such as nut burgers, or nut roast, can be surprisingly economical, as well as healthy and good to eat.

You can buy ready chopped mixed nuts at health food stores and some supermarkets – make sure the supermarket ones aren't sweetened – and these are convenient and reasonably priced. Generally I prefer to buy individual varieties and make my own mixture, and you can usually buy nuts in small quantities to make this possible on a budget. It's best, anyway, only to buy what you can use within a couple of weeks or so, and to buy from a store that has a quick turnover, because nuts can go rancid – and aren't good for you – if kept for too long. Take special care when buying walnuts: if they taste bitter, they're old, and will spoil the flavour of your dish.

Peanuts are cheap and nourishing, but I find you can get tired of them quite quickly and their flavour seems to dominate other nuts, so use carefully. You can buy them in various forms. If you buy the unroasted ones, they are easy to roast at home, and when they're roasted, the skins will just rub off. The same applies to hazelnuts bought with their brown skins still on.

To roast peanuts or hazelnuts: spread the nuts out on a baking tray and bake in a moderate oven for about 20 minutes, or under a hot grill (broiler) for about 10 minutes, until the skins will rub off easily and the nuts underneath are brown. Rub off the skins in a soft cloth.

easy nut burgers

These make a good supper dish, served in soft baps or rolls with sliced tomato and onion. The quantities can easily be multiplied up to serve more people, or halved for one person.

serves 2–4

1 onion, peeled and chopped
1 small celery stalk, finely chopped
25g/1oz/2tbsp butter
$\frac{1}{2}$tsp dried mixed herbs
1$\frac{1}{2}$tsp flour
$\frac{1}{2}$tsp vegetarian stock powder
1$\frac{1}{2}$tsp soy sauce
$\frac{1}{2}$tsp yeast extract
125g/4oz/1 cup mixed nuts – almonds, Brazil nuts, walnuts, cashew nuts, finely chopped or ground in the food processor
6 heaped tbsp soft wholewheat breadcrumbs
sea salt
freshly ground black pepper

To finish
dried breadcrumbs
oil for shallow frying

Fry the onion and celery in the butter for 10 minutes, browning them lightly. Add the herbs, stir for a minute, then mix in the flour and cook for 1–2 minutes. Pour in 5tbsp water and stir until thickened. Add the stock powder, soy sauce, yeast extract, nuts, soft breadcrumbs and salt and pepper to taste. Cool, then form into 4 flat burgers about 1cm/$\frac{1}{2}$ inch thick, and coat with dried breadcrumbs. Pour a little oil into a frying pan, just enough to cover the base thinly, heat, then put in the burgers and fry them until crisp. Turn them over and fry the second side, then drain them on paper towels.

quick nut roast

This is good hot, with a mushroom sauce, or cold with salad and some pickles or chutney. Simply quarter or halve the ingredients to make the right quantity for one or two people, then bake in a small dish for 15–20 minutes for a one-person size, or 20–30 minutes for a two-person roast.

serves 4

Set the oven to 200°C/400°F/Gas 6.

Grease a 20cm/8 inch square pan or a shallow casserole dish. Melt the butter in a large saucepan and fry the onions gently for 10 minutes, until tender. Then add the nuts, breadcrumbs, tomatoes, parsley, dried mixed herbs and lemon juice, and salt and pepper to taste. Press into the prepared container and smooth the top. Bake for 35–40 minutes. Ease the nut roast out of the container, cut into wedges and serve.

25g/1oz/2tbsp butter
2 large onions, peeled and finely chopped
125g/4oz/scant 1 cup cashew nuts, finely chopped or ground in the food processor
125g/4oz/scant 1 cup hazelnuts or almonds, finely chopped or ground in the food processor
12 heaped tbsp soft wholewheat breadcrumbs
2 tomatoes, peeled and chopped
2tbsp chopped fresh parsley
1tsp dried mixed herbs
2tbsp lemon juice
sea salt
freshly ground black pepper

chestnuts

Chestnuts are a cheap and useful food – free, if you pick them up in the woods – their only disadvantage being the rather tedious business of peeling them, which doesn't make them labour-saving. If you feel in the mood for doing them, which is quite fun if there's someone to help you and chat with at the same time, there's a good recipe for using them opposite.

How to peel chestnuts: make a slit in the skin of each chestnut, then either put them into a moderate oven for 10–15 minutes, pop them into a microwave for about 5 minutes, or boil them in water for 10–15 minutes, until the slits are open and you can slip off the skins using a sharp knife and holding the chestnuts in a cloth. The chestnuts will probably be quite soft and 'floury' by this time; if they still seem rather raw, just cover them with a little water and simmer them for about 10 minutes, until soft, then drain.

You can get whole chestnuts ready peeled and cooked in vacuum packs and cans, and you can also buy them frozen. All of these are very good and they save lots of time and trouble – though they're more expensive of course. You can also buy dried chestnuts, but these need soaking for several hours, then simmering gently until very tender. This may take a couple of hours, depending on how hard the chestnuts are, so they're not as convenient. I like the vacuum-packed chestnuts best.

chestnut casserole

If you're using fresh chestnuts and peeling them yourself, you will need about 1kg/2lb in total to get 750g/1½lb when they're peeled; instructions for cooking and peeling them are given on page 104. Cider or wine, replacing some of the stock, makes this warming casserole even better. Cooked Brussels sprouts go well with it, and baked potatoes.

serves 4

Set the oven to 180°C/350°F/Gas 4. Melt the butter in a large saucepan and fry the onion and celery for 10 minutes, but don't brown them; add the garlic, mushrooms and chestnuts and cook for 2–3 minutes. Stir in the flour, then add the tomatoes and stock. Bring up to the boil, then season and transfer to a casserole dish. Bake for 45–60 minutes. Check the seasoning and serve.

25g/1oz/2tbsp butter
1 onion, peeled and chopped
outside stalks from 1 bunch
of celery, sliced
1 clove garlic, crushed
225g/8oz/3 cups
mushrooms, washed
and sliced
750g/1½lb peeled cooked
chestnuts
2tbsp plain (all-purpose)
flour
225g/8oz can tomatoes
600ml/1 pint/2½ cups
vegetable stock
sea salt
freshly ground black pepper

carrot and hazelnut roast

This is extremely quick to make if you've got a food processor, just put everything into it – the carrot and bread cut into chunks – and whizz until smooth. Even without a food processor, this roast is quickly put together and is moist and tasty to eat. I like it best with a salad, but it's also nice with cooked vegetables. I suggest making half this quantity for one person and serving the roast once hot and once cold, with chutney or a sauce made by mixing plain yogurt with mayonnaise and chopped spring (green) onions or fresh herbs.

serves 4 generously

1 large onion, peeled and finely chopped

4 medium-sized carrots, scraped and grated

6 heaped tbsp wholewheat breadcrumbs

225g/8oz/heaping 1½ cups hazelnuts – buy ready skinned ones or buy them in their skins and roast as described on page 101

2tsp dried mixed herbs

2 eggs

1tbsp soy sauce

sea salt

freshly ground black pepper

Set the oven to 190°C/375°F/Gas 5. Line a 900g/2lb loaf pan (measuring about 25 x 13cm/10 x 5 inches) or a deep casserole dish with a long strip of non-stick or greaseproof (waxed) paper to cover the base and go up the narrow sides. Grease well.

Mix all the ingredients together. Spoon the mixture into the container and bake for 45–60 minutes, until firm in the middle and lightly browned. Turn out, ease off the paper, and serve in thick slices.

variations

For a more strongly flavoured roast, add 1–2 crushed cloves garlic and perhaps 1–2tsp yeast extract; a little chopped celery or a pinch or two of celery salt is good in it, too. Or try a curried version: add 2–4tsp curry powder to the basic mixture. Adding 1–2tbsp grated raw ginger is another tasty variation, and so is 1–2tsp chopped fresh rosemary. A mushroomy version is good, too: just add 125–225g/4–8oz/1½–3 cups chopped mushrooms.

Lentils are a useful pulse (legume) because not only are they cheap and tasty, they can also be cooked without soaking, so you don't have to think too far ahead. There are three types of lentils that I think taste good. These are the big greeny-brown whole lentils that are sometimes called green or 'continental' lentils. There's also a whole brown lentil, which is smaller and darker brown. These taste delicious, but I've found that there are often hard pieces of stone mixed in with them, so unless you're prepared to spend time sorting carefully through these lentils, I don't think they are a very good buy. However, similar to look at, and most delicious of all, are the little Puy lentils, which are now quite easy to find. To cook lentils, put them into a saucepan and cover with plenty of cold water – their height again. Bring to the boil and simmer gently, uncovered, for 45–60 minutes, until tender.

The other useful lentils are the split red ones. These cook in only 20 minutes. Put them into a saucepan with a double quantity of water – 1 cup lentils to 2 cups water. Bring to the boil, then cover and cook very gently for 20 minutes, until the lentils are tender and all the water is absorbed. Make sure the heat is low, or the lentils will catch on the bottom of the pan. You can use more water and drain off the excess, but if you're making burgers or a roast from the lentils, use the amount given in the recipe because it's best to have them cooked fairly dry for these, otherwise you seem to need lots of breadcrumbs to make the mixture shapeable.

lentil roast

Very easy, and delicious served in thick slices with a tasty sauce such as vegetarian gravy or tomato sauce. Mint sauce and some roast potatoes are good with it too. To make a roast for one or two people use 1 egg and halve the other ingredients; bake for about 30 minutes.

serves 4

225g/8oz/1 cup split red lentils
400ml/14fl oz/1¾ cups water
1 onion, peeled and finely chopped
25g/1oz/2tbsp butter
1tsp dried mixed herbs
125g/4oz/1 cup grated cheese
1tbsp lemon juice
1 egg, beaten
sea salt
freshly ground black pepper
soft wholewheat breadcrumbs

To finish
wholewheat flour
a little oil

Put the lentils and water into a medium-sized saucepan and simmer very gently, uncovered, until the lentils are tender and all the liquid absorbed, about 20 minutes.

Set the oven to 190°C/375°F/Gas 5. Fry the onion in the butter for 10 minutes until soft and lightly browned, then add this to the lentils together with the dried mixed herbs, cheese, lemon juice, beaten egg and seasoning. Add a few breadcrumbs to stiffen the mixture if necessary. Turn the mixture out on to a board, coat with wholewheat flour and form into a smooth roll shape. Heat a little oil in a pan in the oven; put in the lentil roll and spoon some of the oil over it. Bake for 45 minutes until browned and crisp, basting with oil from time to time.

spicy lentil burgers

Light, delicious and spicy, these are good with either a salad or cooked vegetables. Some hot boiled rice or spiced rice goes well with these, and some mango chutney or lime pickle too. Use a quarter or half of these quantities if you're cooking for one or two people.

serves 4

Put the lentils and water into a medium-sized saucepan and simmer very gently, uncovered, until the lentils are tender and all the liquid is absorbed, about 20 minutes. Fry the chopped onion and green pepper in the butter for 10 minutes until soft, then add the garlic and ginger and cook for a minute or two longer. Add this mixture to the lentils together with the chilli powder, lemon juice and parsley. Season carefully. Form into burger shapes, dip in beaten egg, then into breadcrumbs. Pour enough oil into a frying pan to coat the base and set over a moderate heat. When it's hot, put in the burgers and fry until crisp and brown on one side; turn them over with a palette knife (metal spatula) and cook the other side. Drain on paper towels.

350g/12oz/1¾ cups split red lentils
750ml/1¼ pints/3 cups water
1 large onion, peeled and finely chopped
1 sweet green pepper, deseeded and finely chopped
25g/1oz/2tbsp butter
1 clove garlic, crushed
1tbsp grated fresh ginger
½tsp chilli powder
1tbsp lemon juice
2tbsp chopped fresh parsley
sea salt
freshly ground black pepper

To finish
1 egg, beaten with 1tbsp water
dried breadcrumbs
oil for shallow frying

lentil dal

This is an easy, spicy mixture that goes well with some plain boiled rice and/or some wedges of hardboiled egg. I rather like it with some sliced tomato and watercress or the spiced stuffed tomatoes on page 86; it depends how hungry you're feeling. You can buy creamed coconut in blocks. It keeps for months in the fridge. To make enough dal for two people, halve these ingredients; for one person, use a quarter of these quantities. The cooking time is the same as that given.

serves 4

1 onion, peeled and finely chopped
15g/½oz/1tbsp butter
1 clove garlic, crushed
250g/9oz/1⅓ cups split red lentils
½tsp chilli power
1tsp each ground cumin, turmeric and salt
750ml/1¼ pints/3 cups water
50g/2oz creamed coconut, chopped

Fry the onion in the butter for 10 minutes until soft and lightly browned, then add the garlic, lentils, spices and salt and stir for 2–3 minutes. Add the water and bring to the boil, then simmer gently for 25–30 minutes, until the lentils are tender. Add the creamed coconut and stir over the heat until dissolved. Check the seasoning and serve.

lentils and mushrooms au gratin

In this recipe the lentils are made into a thick sauce which is poured over mushrooms, topped with crumbs and grated cheese and baked until crisp and golden brown. Make a half quantity for two people, or a quarter quantity for one person, baking for 30 minutes or 15 minutes respectively.

serves 4

Put the lentils and milk and water into a medium-sized saucepan and simmer very gently, uncovered, until the lentils are tender and all the liquid absorbed – about 20 minutes.

Set the oven to 180°C/350°F/Gas 4. Meanwhile, melt half the butter and fry the onion for 10 minutes until soft and lightly browned, then add this to the lentils together with the lemon rind and juice, salt, pepper and yeast extract; whizz in the food processor or blender, or beat well with a wooden spoon, to make a thick purée. Fry the mushrooms in the rest of the butter for 2–3 minutes, then put them into a shallow ovenproof dish and pour the lentil mixture on top. Sprinkle with breadcrumbs and grated cheese. Bake for 40–45 minutes, until golden and crisp on top, hot and bubbly underneath.

175g/6oz/scant 1 cup split red lentils
600ml/1 pint/2½ cups milk and water, mixed
50g/2oz/¼ cup butter
1 large onion, peeled and finely chopped
rind and juice of ½ lemon
sea salt
freshly ground black pepper
1tsp yeast extract
125g/4oz/1½ cups mushrooms, washed and sliced
4 heaped tbsp fresh breadcrumbs
4tbsp grated cheese

lentils with tomatoes and thyme

This simple dish is nicest when it is made with fresh tomatoes, although you could use a 400g/14oz can instead. Serve with crusty bread or rolls. If there's any over, it's very pleasant cold, as a salad. To make enough for fewer people, halve the ingredients for two, quarter them for one.

serves 4

225g/8oz/heaping 1 cup green or Puy lentils
25g/1oz/2tbsp butter
2 large onions, peeled and thinly sliced
1 clove garlic, crushed
2–3tsp dried thyme
450g/1lb/2½ cups tomatoes, peeled and chopped
2–3tbsp chopped fresh parsley
sea salt
freshly ground black pepper

Put the lentils into a large saucepan, cover generously with water and boil gently until tender, 45–60 minutes. Drain well.

Melt the butter in a large saucepan and fry the onions until tender. Add the garlic, thyme, tomatoes, drained lentils and parsley. Season with salt and pepper. Reheat gently, and serve.

beautiful beans

Beans are a very useful basic for the thrifty cook. They're healthy, nutritious and can be delicious if they're prepared in an imaginative way. There are many varieties available and it's interesting trying different ones. I've described over thirty of these in my *Bean Book*. For the purposes of this book, I've chosen several tried-and-trusted ones which are easy to buy, and quick and easy to prepare tastily. These are chick peas (garbanzo beans), red kidney beans, butter beans, bean mix, which is a colourful mixture you can get at health food stores and some supermarkets, and split peas.

Chick peas (garbanzo beans), red kidney beans and butter beans can be bought dried or in cans. It's cheaper to buy the dried ones and soak and cook them yourself, and worth it if you're cooking for a number of people and/or have a freezer, so that you can save what you don't need. The canned beans are also a good buy, and can form the basis of some very economical meals.

TO PREPARE DRIED BEANS

Put the beans into a big saucepan and cover them with their height again in cold water; leave to soak for 8 hours. Or bring them to the boil, simmer for 2 minutes, then remove from the heat, cover and leave to stand for 1 hour. Drain and rinse the beans, cover them with fresh water as before, and bring to the boil. Boil them vigorously for 10 minutes, then turn the heat down so that they simmer steadily until tender. That is, 1–1½ hours, although chick peas (garbanzo beans) can be obstinate and sometimes take 3 hours or so to soften. This usually means they are rather old and dried up. They do not keep for ever, so buy from a store with a rapid turnover, and use them up within a few months. Black eyed beans (peas) do not need soaking, although they can be, and they will cook in 30–45 minutes.

TO MICROWAVE BEANS

To do the hot quick soak, put the beans into a bowl with water to cover generously. Cover with a plate. Microwave on full power until the water comes to the boil, then continue to microwave for 1 minute. Allow the beans to stand, covered, for 1 hour.

To cook soaked beans, put them into a bowl with enough water to cover them, cover with a plate, then microwave on full until tender: 45 minutes for 225g/8oz/1⅓ cups red kidney beans and bean mix, followed by 15 minutes standing time, covered; 25 minutes for 225g/8oz/heaping 1 cup chick peas (garbanzo beans), plus 10 minutes standing time; 10 minutes for 225g/8oz/1 cup split peas, plus 10 minutes standing time.

INDIGESTION

If you find that pulses (legumes) give you wind, you might like to try this tip which was sent to me by a Canadian reader. She said that she'd suffered for years, but had found that if she boiled beans and lentils without a lid on the pan, so that all the vapours could get out of the pan, they were perfectly alright and she could eat them every day without any problem.

chick peas in tomato, herb and garlic dressing

Serve this with some crisp lettuce and warm wholewheat rolls for a filling light meal.

Put all the dressing ingredients in a small bowl, or in a screwtop jar, and whisk or shake together. Pour the dressing over the chick peas (garbanzo beans) in a largish bowl and mix well. Leave for 2–3 hours, if possible, for the flavours to be absorbed.

125g/4oz/heaping ½ cup chick peas (garbanzo beans), soaked, cooked and drained, or a 400g/14oz can, rinsed and drained

For the dressing
2tbsp finely chopped onion
1tbsp wine vinegar
1tsp mustard powder
1tsp sugar
2tbsp tomato paste
1tbsp chopped fresh parsley
1tbsp chopped fresh herbs –
if available
1 clove garlic, crushed
3tbsp olive oil
sea salt
freshly ground black pepper

middle eastern chick pea stew

This is easy to make and an excellent dish when aubergines (eggplants) are reasonably priced. Some cooked rice goes well with it. Make a half quantity for two people; for one, it saves time to make a half quantity and serve it once hot and once cold – with a warm, crusty roll, it makes a pleasant salad.

serves 4

olive or groundnut (peanut) oil
2 large onions
1kg/2lb aubergines (eggplants), cut into 1cm/½ inch dice
2 cloves garlic, crushed
400g/14oz can tomatoes
125g/4oz/heaping 1 cup chick peas (garbanzo beans), soaked, cooked and drained, or a 400g/14oz can, drained
sea salt
freshly ground black pepper

Set the oven to 200°C/400°F/Gas 6. Heat a little oil in a large saucepan and fry the onions for 10 minutes. Then remove the onions from the pan with a slotted spoon and fry the aubergine (eggplant) pieces until they're crisp and lightly browned, adding more oil if necessary.

Put the aubergine (eggplant) and onions into an ovenproof dish, together with the garlic, tomatoes, chick peas (garbanzo beans) and some seasoning. Cover and bake for 40–60 minutes.

easy vegetable and red kidney bean stew

serves 4

Heat the oil in a large saucepan and add the onion, red pepper, carrots, leeks or courgettes (zucchini) and celery. Cook gently for 10 minutes, with a lid on the pan, then add the mushrooms, tomatoes, beans, paprika and some salt and pepper to taste. Cook, covered, for a further 10–15 minutes. Check the seasoning. Serve with baked or mashed potatoes, or crusty wholewheat rolls.

1tbsp vegetable oil
1 large onion, sliced
1 large sweet red pepper, deseeded and chopped
2 carrots, scraped and diced
2 leeks or medium-sized courgettes (zucchini), sliced
2 celery stalks, sliced
175g/6oz/2¼ cups mushrooms, washed and sliced
4 tomatoes, peeled and quartered
125g/4oz/⅔ cup red kidney beans, soaked, cooked and drained, or a 400g/14oz can, rinsed and drained
½tsp paprika
sea salt
freshly ground black pepper

red kidney bean and tomato pie

This is a potato-topped pie: simple and quick. A cooked green vegetable such as sprouts or broccoli goes well with it. For two people, simply halve the ingredients and bake the finished pie for 30 minutes; for one person, use a quarter of the quantities – half a 225g/8oz can tomatoes and half a 225g/8oz can red kidney beans – and bake for 20 minutes.

serves 4

2 large onions, peeled and sliced
1tbsp vegetable oil
175g/6oz/2¼ cups mushrooms, washed and sliced – optional
400g/14oz can tomatoes
125g/4oz/⅔ cup red kidney beans, soaked, cooked and drained, or a 400g/14oz can, rinsed and drained
sea salt
freshly ground black pepper
750g/1½lb/4¼ cups creamy mashed potatoes
4tbsp grated cheese

Set the oven to 200°C/400°F/Gas 6. Fry the onions in the oil for 7 minutes, then add the mushrooms, if you're using these, and fry for a further 3 minutes. Remove from the heat and add the tomatoes, beans and seasoning. Spoon the mixture into a shallow ovenproof dish. Spoon the potato on top and spread it evenly, covering all the bean mixture. Sprinkle with the grated cheese. Bake for 30–40 minutes, until golden brown on top.

red kidney bean salad

Put the red kidney beans into a bowl. In another bowl, or
in a screwtop jar, put all the dressing ingredients except
the parsley and whisk or shake together. Pour the
dressing over the beans and mix well. If possible, leave
for 2–3 hours, for the beans to absorb the flavours.
Sprinkle with the parsley just before serving.

125g/4oz/⅔ cup red kidney
beans, soaked, cooked and
drained, or a 400g/14oz
can, rinsed and drained

For the dressing
2tbsp finely chopped onion
1tbsp wine vinegar
1tsp made mustard
1tsp sugar
2tbsp tomato paste
1 clove garlic, crushed
3tbsp olive oil
sea salt
freshly ground black pepper
1tbsp chopped fresh parsley

multicolour beans

For two people, halve all the quantities; for one person, use a quarter of the quantities –
a 225g/8oz can butter beans, or 50g/2oz/heaping ¼ cup dried ones, and 1 celery stalk.

serves 4

3 celery stalks, cut into
6mm/¼ inch dice
1 small sweet red pepper,
deseeded and cut into
6mm/¼ inch dice
1tbsp oil
2tsp curry powder
225g/8oz/heaping 1 cup
frozen sweetcorn kernels
225g/8oz/heaping 1 cup
butter or lima beans,
soaked, cooked and drained,
or two 400g/14oz cans,
rinsed and drained
sea salt
freshly ground black pepper
chopped fresh parsley

Fry the celery and red pepper in the oil in a large saucepan
for 10 minutes, until soft but not browned. Add the curry
powder and stir for 1 minute, then add the sweetcorn
and beans and cook over a gentle heat for 4–5 minutes,
until everything is heated through. Season with salt and
pepper and sprinkle with chopped parsley. Baked potatoes
go well with this, and it's nice cold as well as hot.

beans, peppers and tomatoes au gratin

This is easy, tasty and colourful. For two people, simply halve the ingredients and bake the finished pie for 30 minutes. For one person, use a quarter of the quantities – half a 225g/8oz can tomatoes and half a 225g/8oz can red kidney beans – and bake for 20 minutes.

serves 4

Fry the onions and green pepper in the oil in a large saucepan for 10 minutes, until soft but not browned. Add the garlic, beans, tomatoes and seasoning to taste. Prepare a hot grill (broiler). Put the butter bean mixture into the grill (broiler) pan, or a shallow flameproof dish which will fit under the grill (broiler). Sprinkle the grated cheese evenly over the top. Grill (broil) until the cheese has melted and is golden brown. Serve with crusty bread.

2 large onions, peeled and sliced
1 sweet green pepper, deseeded and sliced
1tbsp oil
1 clove garlic, crushed
225g/8oz/heaping 1 cup dried butter or lima beans, soaked, cooked and drained, or two 400g/14oz cans, rinsed and drained
400g/14oz can tomatoes
sea salt
freshly ground black pepper
125g/4oz/1 cup grated cheese

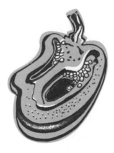

technicolour bean salad

For this recipe I love the pretty colours of the 'bean mix' which you can get at health food stores and some supermarkets, but you could make up your own by mixing equal quantities of, say, red kidney beans, black beans, flageolet beans, black eyed beans (peas) and pinto beans. Make up a quarter or half of this mixture for one or two people.

serves 4

225g/8oz/1⅓ cups 'bean mix' or any mixture of beans
1 medium-sized mild onion, peeled and finely chopped
1 clove garlic, crushed
½tsp made mustard
1tbsp red wine vinegar
3tbsp olive oil
sea salt
freshly ground black pepper
4tbsp chopped fresh parsley

Soak the beans in plenty of cold water overnight. Next day, drain and rinse them, then put them into a saucepan with their height again in cold water and bring to the boil. Boil the beans hard for 10 minutes, then turn the heat down and let them simmer for 1 hour or so until they are all tender.

Drain the beans and add the onion. Mix together the garlic, mustard, vinegar, oil and a little salt and pepper; add this to the bean mixture and stir well. Leave the beans to cool, stirring from time to time, then add the parsley. Serve with crusty rolls, or on a base of lettuce.

Grains are cheap and nourishing. Although we usually think of them as starch 'fillers', they actually contain quite a lot of protein, as well as B vitamins, and minerals such as iron, so they can easily become main courses. They're also very easy to cook.

There are quite a number of grains and although rice is probably the most useful, it's worth trying some of the more unusual ones such as millet and bulgur wheat, which you can get at the health food store, for variety. Leftover grains are useful because they make a good base for rissoles, stuffings or salads – just add small quantities of tasty ingredients such as fried onions or mushrooms, garlic and herbs, chopped hardboiled egg or nuts, and you've practically got another meal.

Rice for savoury dishes should be the long-grained variety, and you don't need to pay extra for treated, quick-cooking or easy-cook rice. All rice is easy to cook, and you shouldn't find you have any problems. I prefer brown rice because of its nutty flavour and chewy texture, and the extra B vitamins and fibre it contains.

BASIC COOKING OF BROWN RICE

There are two methods, and each have their devotees, but I think both work equally well, so it's really a question of which one you like best.

The fast-boiling, lots of water, method

For this method you need to half fill a large saucepan with water, bring to the boil and add 1tsp salt. Throw in the rice, allowing 50g/2oz/heaping ¼ cup per person if the rice is to accompany something else, or up to 125g/4oz/heaping ½ cup each if the rice is more or less the main dish, without much else. Let the rice boil away, without a lid on the pan, for 20–30 minutes, until the rice is tender. Drain the rice into a colander and rinse it under hot running water to remove any starch. Tip it back into the saucepan and dry over a low heat for about 5 minutes, stirring to prevent sticking. The rice can also be dried off – and kept warm – in a cool oven. Put the rice into a shallow ovenproof dish and place, uncovered, in the oven for about 10 minutes.

The slow-cook, not much water, method

For this you need to measure both the rice and the water, and it's handy to use the same container for this – a large mug or a cup measure. Choose a medium-sized saucepan which has a close-fitting lid, if possible. You can fry an onion in a tablespoonful of oil before putting in the rice, and spices such as cloves, turmeric and cinnamon stick can be added too, for a spiced rice. Put one measure of rice into the saucepan, on top of the onion, if you're using this, and add two measures of water and 1tsp salt. Bring to the boil, then put the lid on the pan – or cover closely with a piece of foil and/or an old plate – and turn the heat down as low as it will go. Leave the rice, without peeking or stirring, until it's tender and all the water has been absorbed, which takes 45 minutes.

To cook rice in the microwave

Put the rice into a microwave-proof container with water and a little salt, using the proportions of 1 cup rice to 2 cups water. Cover with a plate. Microwave on full power, without stirring, for 25 minutes. Leave to stand, still covered, for 10 minutes, then fluff up with a fork.

rice salad

Rice salad is easy to make and can be exactly what you want it to be: just add the ingredients to the cooked rice. The more contrast you can get in the colour, texture and flavour of the ingredients you add, the better. Chopped raw onion or spring (green) onion, small cubes of cucumber and chopped red or sweet green pepper are good additions, so too are cooked sweetcorn kernels, cooked peas, small cubes of cooked carrot or coarsely grated raw carrot, finely chopped celery, raisins or sultanas (golden raisins), finely chopped dried apricots, chopped nuts, chopped peeled tomato, cooked red kidney beans and chick peas (garbanzo beans), black olives and chopped fresh herbs.

A lightly curried rice salad is nice too: you make this by frying an onion in some oil with a little curry powder and stirring that into the rice, together with some diced apple, sliced banana, roasted peanuts and finely chopped hardboiled eggs. Once you have added your chosen ingredients, moisten the mixture with a little vinaigrette dressing or a spoonful or two of some good-quality mayonnaise thinned with milk. Check the seasoning, then spoon the salad into a serving dish and garnish with some chopped parsley, chives or black olives.

provençal gratin

This delicious recipe was given to me by a French friend and is an old family one from Provence. Make half these quantities for one or two people. If there's any over, it's good cold with salad, or as a filling for sweet green peppers or big tomatoes. See pages 82 and 86 for how to prepare these.

serves 3–4

225g/8oz/heaping 1 cup brown rice
1 large onion, peeled and chopped
4 courgettes (zucchini), diced
2tbsp oil
125g/4oz/1 cup grated cheese
1 egg
sea salt
freshly ground black pepper

Cook the rice until tender – see page 124. Meanwhile, set the oven to 180°C/350°F/Gas 4 and fry the onion and courgettes (zucchini) in the oil for 15–20 minutes, until very soft.

Drain the rice if necessary, and add to the onion and courgettes (zucchini) with half the cheese, the egg and salt and pepper to taste. Mix well. Spoon the mixture into a shallow ovenproof dish, sprinkle with the rest of the cheese and bake in the oven for about 45 minutes, or longer if you like: this is delicious really well cooked to a deep golden brown. It goes well with a sliced tomato salad or some green salad.

vegetable rice with roasted nuts

If you're cooking for two people, use half these quantities; for one person, I suggest using half the quantities and serving this once hot with a salad, and once cold with hot garlic bread.

serves 4

Fry the onion in the olive oil in a large saucepan for 10 minutes, until soft but not browned, then add the turmeric and garlic. Stir, then add the rice, water and salt. Bring up to the boil, then turn the heat right down and put a lid on the pan. Cook for 20 minutes.

After 20 minutes, lift off the lid and put the carrot, red pepper and green beans or leeks on top of the rice – don't stir them in. Cover and cook for another 20 minutes. Then add the tomatoes, some freshly ground pepper and the roasted nuts. Stir gently to mix everything together. Serve at once, sprinkled with chopped parsley. This is nice with a simple salad, such as watercress. If there's any over, it's lovely cold – or it can be used to stuff peppers.

variation

Use a can of drained red kidney beans instead of the nuts – add them with the tomatoes.

1 onion, peeled and chopped
1tbsp olive oil
½tsp turmeric
1 clove garlic, crushed
225g/8oz/heaping 1 cup brown rice
400ml/14fl oz/1¾ cups water
1tsp salt
1 large carrot, scraped and diced
1 sweet red pepper, deseeded and chopped
225g/8oz green beans or leeks, cut into 2.5cm/1 inch pieces
4 tomatoes, peeled and sliced
freshly ground black pepper
124g/4 oz/scant 1 cup roasted nuts – peanuts or cashew nuts
chopped fresh parsley

curried rice and eggs

This is simple, but very good, and if you plan ahead and cook your rice beforehand it is very quick to make. Use half these quantities for two people, quarter quantities for one, which means using 3tsp flour for the sauce.

serves 4

350–450g/12oz–1lb/2–2⅔ cups cooked rice
6 hardboiled eggs, shelled and sliced
50g/2oz/¼ cup butter
1–2tsp curry powder
2 rounded tbsp plain (all-purpose) flour
600ml/1 pint/2½ cups milk
sea salt
freshly ground black pepper
a drop or two of Tabasco

Put the rice and eggs into a shallow casserole dish and warm them through in a 170°C/325°F/Gas 3 oven. Make a sauce: melt the butter in a medium-sized saucepan and stir in the curry powder and flour; cook for a moment or two, then add the milk and stir over the heat until smooth. Let the sauce simmer over a gentle heat for 10–15 minutes, to cook the flour. Then season with salt, pepper and Tabasco to taste. Pour the sauce over the rice and eggs and serve piping hot. If there's any over, it makes excellent croquettes.

spiced rice

Some spiced rice makes a pleasant, money-saving meal, served either just with a tomato salad or with a curry sauce – see overleaf. The ingredients can be halved; the cooking time remains the same.

serves 4 with a curry, 2 as a main course with salad

Heat the oil or butter in a medium-sized saucepan, then add the rice. Fry the rice over a gentle heat for 5 minutes, stirring. Then add the spices and some salt and pepper and stir for 1–2 minutes. Finally add the water – stand back, it will sizzle – and bring up to the boil. Cover the pan, turn the heat down and leave to cook very gently for 45 minutes, after which time all the water should have been absorbed. If it hasn't, just leave the rice to stand, covered but off the heat, for a further 10–15 minutes. Fluff the rice by stirring gently with a fork, and serve.

1tbsp oil or butter
225g/8oz/heaping 1 cup brown rice
1tsp turmeric
3 cloves
2–3 cardamom pods – if available
2.5cm/1 inch piece of cinnamon stick – if available
sea salt
freshly ground black pepper
600ml/1 pint/2½ cups boiling water

curry sauce for rice

This curry sauce can be used over plain boiled rice or spiced rice – see page 129. It can also be used as a base for any vegetables which you may have. Halve the amount for one or two people.

serves 4

25g/1oz/2tbsp butter
1 large onion, peeled and chopped
a walnut-sized piece of fresh ginger, grated
2 cloves garlic, crushed
1 bayleaf
1tbsp ground coriander
1tbsp ground cumin
pinch of chilli powder
225g/8oz can tomatoes
1tsp salt
freshly ground black pepper
600ml/1 pint/2½ cups water

Heat the butter in a large saucepan and fry the onion for 7–8 minutes, then add the ginger, garlic, bayleaf and spices and stir over the heat for 2–3 minutes. Add the tomatoes, salt, some pepper and the water. Let the sauce simmer gently for about 30 minutes.

If you're adding raw vegetables, such as cubes of potato or slices of carrot, put them in with the tomatoes; quicker-cooking vegetables, such as cauliflower, peas or a little shredded white cabbage, and also leftover cooked vegetables, are best added about 10 minutes before the end of the cooking time.

variation

For egg curry, add 4–6 shelled and quartered hardboiled eggs to the curry sauce about 10 minutes before you serve the curry and sprinkle with some desiccated (dried shredded) coconut.

rice croquettes

These are delicious, crisp on the outside and tender inside. Serve them with some sliced tomatoes and mango chutney, or with a sauce made by stirring some chopped fresh herbs or spring (green) onion into some plain yogurt. Use half these quantities to make enough for one or two people, with half a beaten egg to bind and half to coat the outside of the croquettes.

serves 3–4

Mix together the rice, hardboiled eggs, parsley, grated cheese and raw egg. Add enough curry powder to give the mixture a spicy lift, ½–1tsp perhaps, and salt and pepper to taste. Form the mixture into croquettes about the size of golf balls, dip them into beaten egg, then into dried crumbs. Pour enough oil into a frying pan to cover the base lightly and set over a moderate heat. When the oil is hot, put in the croquettes and fry them, turning them around with a palette knife (metal spatula) so that they get browned all over. Drain them on paper towels. Serve at once.

350g/12oz/2 cups cooked rice

2 hardboiled eggs, shelled and finely chopped

2tbsp chopped fresh parsley

4tbsp grated cheese

1 egg

curry powder

sea salt

freshly ground black pepper

To finish
1 egg, beaten with 1tbsp cold water

dried crumbs

oil for shallow frying

oats

Rolled oats – the ordinary 'porridge' oats which you can buy at any supermarket – can be used to make a quick and easy savoury. You can also make your own homemade muesli mix from these much more cheaply, and I think better, than buying a made-up one. Just put 2 cupfuls of rolled oats into a bowl, add $^1/_2$ cup raisins and $^1/_2$ cup nuts and mix together. The nicest nuts to use, I think, are hazelnuts. Buy the kind which still have their skins on – from health food stores – and roast them as described on page 101, then chop them coarsely.

quick oat savoury

This couldn't be quicker or easier. For one person, halve the quantities and bake for about 20 minutes. For four people, double the ingredients and bake for about 40 minutes.

serves 2

4 heaped tbsp rolled oats

450g/1lb/2$^1/_2$ cups tomatoes, peeled and chopped, plus 3–4tbsp milk, or

a 400g/14oz can

125g/4oz/1 cup grated cheese

Set the oven to 200°C/400°F/Gas 6. Grease a shallow ovenproof dish. Put half the oats in the dish, followed by half the tomatoes, then half the grated cheese. Repeat the layers. Sprinkle with the milk if you're using fresh tomatoes. Bake for 30 minutes, until the oats have absorbed the moisture and the dish is golden brown on top. A crunchy salad, such as cabbage and carrot, goes well with this.

barley

Barley is cheap and has a pleasant flavour. The kind of barley I prefer is pearl barley, which you can get at any supermarket. Although this has been refined to some extent, it still contains a lot of fibre, and is actually a better source of this than brown rice. You can cook it in the same way as rice and serve it as an accompaniment or the basis of a main dish or salad, with other vegetables and flavourings added. I think it's nicest in its more traditional role, as a filling ingredient in soups and stews.

barley casserole

serves 4

Peel and chop the onion. Scrape and slice the carrots. Wash the leeks and cut them into 2.5cm/1 inch chunks. Peel the potatoes and cut into 2.5cm/1 inch chunks. Crush the garlic. Heat the oil in a large saucepan. Add the onion and fry for 5 minutes, then put in the carrots, leeks, potatoes and garlic and fry for a further 5 minutes. Add the barley, stir well, then add the water and stock powder. Bring to the boil, then simmer for abut 30 minutes, until the vegetables and barley are tender. Add the soy sauce and mushrooms and cook for 4–5 minutes, then check the seasoning. Serve sprinkled with chopped parsley.

1 large onion
4 large carrots
450g/1lb leeks
2 large potatoes
2 cloves garlic
2tbsp oil
125g/4oz/heaping ½ cup pearl barley
1 litre/1¾ pints/1 quart water
1tbsp vegetarian stock powder
2tbsp soy sauce
125–225g/4–8oz/1½–3 cups mushrooms, sliced
sea salt
freshly ground black pepper
chopped fresh parsley

millet

Millet makes a pleasant change from rice. You can buy it at health food stores and it's useful if you're anaemic, as it's a good source of iron. You can cook it exactly like rice, using the slow-cook method, and the millet will only take 20 minutes. It tastes best if you roast it a bit before adding the water – see the beginning of the pilaf recipe below.

spicy millet pilaf

Serve this with a crunchy salad. If there's any over, add an egg and make the mixture into flat burgers, then coat in beaten egg and crumbs and shallow fry.

serves 4

350g/12oz/1½ cups millet
2tbsp oil
1 large onion, peeled and chopped
2 carrots, diced
1 clove garlic, crushed
a walnut-sized piece of fresh ginger, grated
2.5cm/1 inch piece of cinnamon stick
750ml/1¼ pints/3 cups water
sea salt
freshly ground black pepper

Put the millet into a large saucepan and stir over a moderate heat for 3–4 minutes, until it begins to smell roasted and some of the grains start to pop. Remove from the heat and tip into a bowl. Heat the oil in the saucepan and fry the onion and carrots for about 7 minutes. Add the garlic, ginger and cinnamon and stir for a moment or two, then stir in the millet. Add the water and some salt and pepper. Bring to the boil, then cover and cook very gently for 15–20 minutes until the water is absorbed. Fluff the millet with a fork.

buckwheat

Buckwheat has a strong flavour, and it's an economical, healthy grain, so it's certainly worth a try. Buy roasted buckwheat, which you can get at health food stores, and cook it by the slow-cook rice method. Flavour it with onion, garlic and soy sauce. Mushrooms and carrots also go well with buckwheat, as in this recipe.

buckwheat hotpot

Serve this with a cooked green vegetable, such as Brussels sprouts or spinach.

serves 4

Peel and chop the onions. Slice the carrots into rings. Crush the garlic. Wash and chop the mushrooms. Heat the oil in the saucepan and fry the onions and carrots for about 7 minutes. Add the garlic and mushrooms and fry for 2–3 minutes, then add the buckwheat, herbs, water and some salt and pepper. Bring to the boil, then cover and leave to cook gently for 30 minutes, until all the water has been absorbed and the carrots are tender. Add the soy sauce and parsley, check the seasoning and serve.

2 large onions
450g/1lb carrots
1 clove garlic
125g/4oz/1½ cups mushrooms
2tbsp oil
225g/8oz/1 cup roasted buckwheat
2tsp dried mixed herbs
300ml/10fl oz/1¼ cups water
sea salt
freshly ground black pepper
2tbsp soy sauce
2tbsp chopped fresh parsley

bulgur wheat

This is sometimes called burghul wheat and is a pre-cooked grain, so it doesn't need much cooking. In fact it can just be soaked, 1 cup wheat to 2 cups hot or cold water, left for 10–15 minutes until the water has been absorbed, then used. You can make a very good Middle Eastern salad, tabbouleh, by adding peeled and chopped tomatoes, chopped raw onion and lots of chopped fresh parsley and mint, and some lemon juice, olive oil, salt and pepper to soaked bulgur wheat. For most savoury dishes, however, the wheat needs to be heated after soaking; you can do this by putting it into a greased ovenproof dish and heating it in a moderate oven, or you can do the soaking and cooking processes in one go by cooking the wheat by the slow-cook rice method.

bulgur pilaf with red lentils

serves 4

1 large onion
2 tbsp oil
2 cloves garlic
a piece of fresh ginger
225g/8oz/1⅓ cups bulgur wheat
125g/4oz/heaping ½ cup split red lentils
sea salt
freshly ground black pepper
2 heaped tbsp chopped fresh parsley
1 tbsp lemon juice

Peel and chop the onion and fry it in the oil in a medium-sized saucepan for about 7 minutes. Crush the garlic and grate the ginger, then stir them into the onion for a moment or two. Add the bulgur wheat and lentils and stir, then pour in 600ml/1 pint/2½ cups water and add some salt and pepper. Bring to the boil, then cover and turn down the heat. Cook very gently for 30 minutes, until all the water is absorbed and the lentils are pale and tender. Gently stir in the parsley with a fork, then add the lemon juice and salt and pepper to taste.

nutty bulgur pilaf

Less liquid than usual is used – 1½ times the amount of grain instead of 2 times – because of the moisture the vegetables contribute. Use half quantities for one or two servings.

serves 3–4

Fry the onion and red pepper in the oil in a medium-sized saucepan for about 7 minutes. Then add the garlic, ginger and cinnamon and stir for a moment or two. Add the bulgur wheat and stir, then pour in the water and add some salt and pepper. Bring up to the boil, then cover the saucepan, turn down the heat and leave to cook very gently for 10–15 minutes, until all the water has been absorbed. Fluff with a fork and add the nuts and raisins.

1 large onion, peeled and chopped
1 sweet red pepper, deseeded and chopped
2tbsp oil
1 clove garlic, crushed
a walnut-sized piece of fresh ginger, grated
2.5cm/1 inch piece of cinnamon stick – if available
225g/8oz/1⅓ cups bulgur wheat
300ml/10fl oz/1¼ cups water
sea salt
freshly ground black pepper
50g/2oz/⅔ cup flaked almonds – or roasted peanuts for economy
50g/2oz/scant ½ cup raisins

semolina

Semolina makes the basis of two delicious savoury dishes, definite 'stars' in the thrifty cook's repertoire. If you want to make both dishes from one batch of mixture, use the basic mixture given for cheese fritters, spread it out and leave until cold. Use half the mixture for the fritters and cut the rest into circles for the gnocchi.

italian gnocchi

This is a little more trouble than some of the dishes in this book, but it can be made in stages and is cheap and delicious.

serves 4

600ml/1 pint/2½ cups milk
4 heaped tbsp semolina
1 small egg
75g/3oz/¾ cup grated Parmesan cheese
sea salt
freshly ground black pepper
grated nutmeg
15g/½oz/1tbsp butter

Put the milk into a large saucepan and bring to the boil. Sprinkle the semolina gradually over the milk, beating well after each addition – a wire balloon whisk is good for this. When all the semolina has been added, simmer gently for 5 minutes. Remove from the heat and beat in the egg and two thirds of the cheese. Season with salt, pepper and nutmeg. Spread the mixture into a lightly oiled shallow pan or on to a plate, so that it is 8mm/⅓ inch deep. Leave to get completely cold, then cut into squares, or into circles using a pastry cutter. Put the trimmings into a shallow dish, then arrange the gnocchi on top. Dot with the butter, sprinkle with the remaining cheese and put under a hot grill (broiler) until the top is golden brown and the inside heated through. This is good served with a watercress or tomato salad.

cheese fritters

These are a bit fiddly to make, though you can do them in stages. They are cheap and delicious. I usually serve them with homemade parsley sauce, made as described on page 12. Even if you're cooking for one or two people, I recommend making the full quantity and freezing what you don't eat. If not, these quantities will halve or quarter satisfactorily.

serves 4

Put the milk, onion and bayleaf into a saucepan and bring the milk to the boil. Remove from the heat, cover and leave for 10–15 minutes, for the flavours to infuse. Remove the onion and bayleaf. Bring the milk back to the boil, then sprinkle the semolina over the top, stirring all the time. Let the mixture simmer for about 5 minutes, to cook the semolina, then remove from the heat and beat in the cheese, mustard and seasoning to taste. Spread the mixture out on an oiled plate or baking tray so that it's about 1cm/½ inch deep. Smooth the top, then leave until completely cold. Cut into pieces; dip each first in beaten egg and then in dried crumbs. Shallow fry in hot oil until crisp on both sides, then drain well on paper towels. Serve at once, garnished with lemon slices and parsley sprigs.

600ml/1 pint/2½ cups milk
1 small onion, peeled and stuck with 3–4 cloves
1 bayleaf
4 heaped tbsp semolina
125g/4oz/1 cup grated cheese
½tsp mustard powder
sea salt
freshly ground black pepper

To finish
1 large egg, beaten with 1tbsp water
dried crumbs
oil for shallow frying
slices of lemon
sprigs of parsley

couscous

A pre-cooked grain, actually a type of semolina, couscous is very easy to use. It only needs to be soaked in hot water, 1 cup couscous to 2 cups water, for about 10 minutes, until all the water has been absorbed, then heated through. The easiest way to do this is to put the couscous into a steamer, metal colander or sieve (strainer) set over a saucepan of steaming stew. The couscous is then served with the stew.

couscous with spicy stew

serves 4

450g/1lb/2⅔ cups couscous
2 onions
225g/8oz carrots
4tbsp olive oil
2tsp each ground cinnamon, cumin and coriander
4tbsp tomato paste
225g/8oz/2 cups courgettes (zucchini), diced
125g/4oz/heaping ½ cup raisins or sweetcorn kernels
225g/8oz/heaping 1 cup dried chick peas (garbanzo beans), soaked, cooked and drained, or two 400g/14oz cans, drained
900ml/1½ pints/3¾ cups water
sea salt
freshly ground black pepper

Soak the couscous in 600ml/1pint/2½cups hot water for 10 minutes. Peel and chop the onions. Scrape and dice the carrots.

Heat 2tbps oil in a large saucepan or the saucepan part of a steamer, add the onions and carrots and fry gently for 10 minutes, then stir in the spices and tomato paste and cook for 2–3 minutes, stirring. Put in the courgettes (zucchini), raisins or sweetcorn, chick peas (garbanzo beans) and water. Bring to the boil, then turn the heat down so that the stew just simmers. By this time the couscous will have absorbed all the water. Put it into the steamer, metal colander or sieve (strainer), breaking it up a bit with your fingers again as you do so. Put the couscous over the stew, cover and leave for 25–30 minutes. Season to taste, stir in the remaining oil, then put the couscous on to a warmed dish and pour the stew into the middle. Sprinkle with some chopped fresh parsley and serve at once.

When you're trying to save money, desserts and puddings somehow become more important. For one thing, they turn a cheap and rather 'thin' dish into a complete meal. Potato soup, for instance, followed by rhubarb crumble; or baked potatoes followed by apple charlotte, or nutty cabbage salad with baked egg custard afterwards. Fresh fruit, of course, always make a quick, easy and healthy dessert and can work out very cheaply if you buy fruit in season.

dreamy desserts

fruit salad

This can be made with whatever fruit is in season and the best value: aim for a pretty mixture of colours. If you're making this for two people, halve the ingredients; for one person, quarter the ingredients, leaving out either the apple or the orange.

serves 4

2 oranges
225g/8oz strawberries, hulled and washed, or black grapes, halved and deseeded, or blackberries or raspberries
2 kiwi fruit, peeled and sliced into rounds, or 1–2 bananas, peeled and sliced
2 apples, cored and sliced, unpeeled if skin is good
150ml/5fl oz/⅔ cup orange or apple juice

Holding the oranges over a bowl and using a sharp knife, cut away the peel and white pith, using a sawing action and cutting round and round as if peeling an apple to produce a long piece of peel. Then cut the orange sections away from the white inner skin. Put the orange sections into the bowl and add the rest of the fruit and the orange or apple juice. Serve plain, or with thick yogurt.

baked apples

These are beautifully easy and cheap when apples are in season. Try filling the cavities with different ingredients: a mixture of ripe blackberries and brown sugar is delicious, so is clear honey mixed with ground almonds, or whole cooking dates, or raisins or sultanas (golden raisins).

Wash the apple and remove the core, leaving the apple whole. Using a sharp knife, score round the apple, just cutting the skin, so that when the apple expands during cooking, the skin won't burst.

Set the oven to 180°C/350°F/Gas 4. Put the apples into a lightly greased ovenproof dish or baking pan and fill the cavities with your chosen ingredients, packing them in well. Bake for 45–60 minutes, until the apples are soft and puffed up. Serve hot, with milk, plain yogurt or single (light) cream.

1 large cooking (tart) apple per person
filling ingredients as suggested above

stewed fruit

This basic recipe works equally well for smaller quantities of fruit than the quantity given here – just halve or quarter the amounts as necessary.

serves 4

1kg/2lb fruit – cooking (tart) apples, peeled, cored and sliced; rhubarb, cut into chunks; gooseberries or blackcurrants, topped and tailed; blackberries; plums, halved and stoned (pitted)
15g/¹/₂oz/1tbsp butter – for apples only
50g/2oz/heaping ¼ cup sugar

Put the fruit into a saucepan with 2tbsp water or, if you're using apples, with the butter instead, and the sugar. Cook over a very gentle heat, covered, until the fruit is tender. Allow 7–10 minutes for apples and soft fruits; up to 15 minutes for firm fruits such as plums. Taste and add more sugar if necessary. Serve hot, warm or cold.

variations

Apple purée: beat stewed apples with a wooden spoon, or, for a smoother result, push through a sieve (strainer).
Stewed dried fruit: allow 125g/4oz/heaping ½ cup for each person. I prefer to use real dried fruit from a health food store – little Hunza apricots are particularly sweet and delicious. Wash the fruit, cover with boiling water and leave to soak overnight. Next day, put the fruit and water into a saucepan, bring to the boil and then cook gently for 20–30 minutes, until the fruit is tender and the liquid is reduced and syrupy. Remove from the heat and use hot or cold. For a boozy version, add a splash of brandy when the fruits are hot but not boiling.

fruit fool

This can be made from any of the stewed fruit bases described on the page opposite.

serves 4–6

Purée the fruit in the food processor or blender, or by pushing it through a nylon sieve (strainer). Or just mash it well. Mix the fruit with the yogurt or custard to make a thick, creamy mixture. Sweeten as necessary. Whisk the cream until it is softly peaking but not too stiff, then gently fold this into the fruit mixture.

1kg/2lb fruit, stewed as described opposite – rhubarb or gooseberries are especially good
300ml/10fl oz/1¼ cups plain yogurt or stove-top egg custard – see page 156
honey or sugar to taste
150ml/5fl oz/⅔ cup whipping cream

fruit meringue

This is delicious if it is cooked very slowly, so that the meringue dries out and becomes crisp. Make half these quantities for two people; for one person, use a quarter of the quantity of stewed fruit and half the amount of meringue topping. Bake these smaller ones for about 1 hour.

serves 4

1kg/2lb fruit, stewed as described on page 144 – rhubarb or apples are especially good

2 eggs, separated

2 rounded tbsp demerara sugar

Set the oven to 150°C/300°F/Gas 2. Mash the stewed fruit so that it has a smoothish texture, then add the egg yolks. Put the mixture into a shallow ovenproof casserole. Whisk the egg whites until they are stiff and glossy, then whisk in the sugar. Spoon this on top of the fruit, spreading it across the dish so that it reaches the edge all round and no fruit is visible. If you leave gaps, steam will come up from the fruit and the meringue won't get nice and crisp. Bake for 1–1½ hours, until the meringue is crisp and sounds hollow when you tap it lightly. Serve hot or cold.

veiled country lass

This is a Danish pudding which consists of layers of crisp crumbs and apple purée. It's served cold with a topping of whipped cream, or plain yogurt if you prefer.

serves 4

To make the crumb layer, melt the butter in a large saucepan or frying pan, add the crumbs and sugar and fry gently, stirring often, until the crumbs are brown and crisp. Remove from the heat and add the grated chocolate and cinnamon; stir until the chocolate has melted. Put a layer of crumbs into the bottom of a serving bowl – glass is nice – then put a layer of apple purée on top of that. Continue in layers until all the apple and crumbs have been used, ending with crumbs. Cool, then chill. Just before you want to serve the pudding, spread the cream or yogurt over the top and decorate, if you like, with some little dollops of raspberry jam.

apple purée made from 1kg/2lb apples – see page 144

For the crumb layers
50g/2oz/¼ cup butter
12 heaped tbsp soft wholewheat breadcrumbs
2tbsp demerara sugar
3tbsp grated plain (semisweet) chocolate
½tsp ground cinnamon
150ml/5fl oz/⅔ cup whipping cream, whipped
2-3tbsp raspberry jam – optional

apple charlotte

Another apple and crumb pudding, this time the British version. It is served hot, with some cream or plain yogurt.

serves 4

grated rind of a well-scrubbed lemon

apple purée made from 1kg/2lb cooking (tart) apples – see page 144

For the crumbs

50g/2oz/¼ cup butter

12 heaped tbsp soft wholewheat breadcrumbs

4tbsp demerara sugar

½tsp ground cinnamon

Set the oven to 190°C/375°F/Gas 5. Add the grated lemon rind to the apple purée. To make the crumb layer, melt the butter in a large saucepan or frying pan, add the crumbs and half the sugar and fry gently, stirring often, until the crumbs are brown and crisp. Remove from the heat and add the cinnamon. Butter a fairly deep ovenproof dish and sprinkle two thirds of the crumb mixture into it, pressing it up the sides of the dish. Spoon the apple mixture on top and sprinkle with the remaining crumbs and the rest of the sugar. Bake for 40–45 minutes, until golden brown and crisp. Serve hot.

summer pudding

You can make this any size you like: a mini one for one person, using a quarter of these ingredients; or a half size for two. Cut the bread thin for the smaller puddings, as there will be more bread in proportion to fruit than with a larger pudding.

serves 6

Put the apples into a large saucepan with the butter and simmer gently, covered, for about 10 minutes, until the apples are tender. Then put in the red fruit, removing the stones (pits) from the plums first if you're using these. Bring to the boil and simmer gently until the fruit is tender. Sweeten to taste. Remove from the heat.

Grease a medium-sized pudding bowl. Cut a piece of bread to fit over the base of the bowl; dip the bread in the fruit so that it soaks up the juice and becomes completely stained red, then press it into the bottom of the bowl. If there isn't enough juice to soak the bread, stir in a small cupful of boiling water. Prepare the rest of the bread in the same way, cutting it to fit round the sides of the bowl so that it is completely lined with bread, which can overlap a bit; don't leave any gaps. Spoon in the fruit, draining off the juice so that the pudding won't be too liquid. When the bowl is full, cover with more soaked bread and a small plate or saucer. Stand a weight on top. Stand the bowl on a plate to catch any drips and leave in the fridge or a cool place overnight. Next day, loosen the edges of the pudding with a palette knife (metal spatula) and turn the pudding out. Serve with whipped cream or thick plain yogurt.

225g/8oz/2 cups cooking (tart) apples, peeled and sliced
15g/½oz/1tbsp butter
750g–1kg/1½–2lb red fruit such as raspberries, redcurrants, blackcurrants, strawberries, plums, blackberries, bilberries or blueberries
sugar
about 8 slices of bread, crusts removed

bread and butter pudding

These quantities can be doubled if you're serving four people: increase the cooking time to 45–50 minutes. Or halve the ingredients for one person and use 1 small egg, then cook for about 15–20 minutes.

serves 2

2 thin slices of stale bread, buttered, and crusts removed
2 heaped tbsp raisins or sultanas (golden raisins)
1 egg
150ml/5fl oz/⅔ cup milk

To finish
a little demerara sugar
a little butter

Set the oven to 170°C/325°F/Gas 3. Cut the slices of bread into four. Layer the bread in a shallow ovenproof dish with the raisins or sultanas (golden raisins), ending with a layer of bread. Beat the egg with the milk and pour this over the bread. Sprinkle a little sugar on top and dot with a few pieces of butter. Bake for 30–40 minutes, until the pudding is set.

sponge pudding

You can make a mini pudding as a treat for one person by using a quarter of these quantities and cooking it in a tiny bowl or an old cup.

serves 4

If you're using the oven, set it to 180°C/350°F/Gas 4 and grease a shallow ovenproof dish. To microwave or steam the pudding, grease a medium-sized pudding bowl. In any case, put the jam or syrup into the base. Sift the flour and baking powder into a bowl, or into your food processor, and add the butter, sugar and eggs. Beat for 1–2 minutes, or whizz for a few seconds, until thick, smooth and slightly glossy. Spoon into the dish or bowl on top of the jam or syrup.

Bake for about 20 minutes, or until the sponge has risen and feels firm to the touch. Or cover the bowl with a plate and microwave for 5–7 minutes, until the sponge has risen and a skewer inserted into the middle comes out with no raw mixture on it. To steam the pudding, cover the bowl with foil, tie with string and stand the bowl in a saucepan containing enough boiling water to come halfway up the bowl. Simmer for 1½ hours, topping the water level up with more boiling water if it gets too low.

To serve, turn the pudding out of the bowl on to a warmed plate, or serve it from the baking dish.

2 heaped tbsp jam or syrup
125g/4oz/¾ cup + 2tbsp self-raising wholewheat flour or a half-and-half mix of white and wholewheat self-raising flour
1tsp baking powder
125g/4oz/½ cup soft butter
125g/4oz/heaping ½ cup caster (superfine) sugar
2 eggs

fruit crumble

A fruit crumble is always popular and is easy to make. Apples and hard pears need to be cooked first, as described on page 144, but this isn't necessary for most other fruits. Rhubarb, plums, soft sweet pears, gooseberries, bilberries, blueberries and blackcurrants can be put straight into the dish, making these quick to prepare. Use half or a third of these ingredients to make a crumble for two people and bake for 20–30 minutes; for one person, use 175g/6oz fruit and 1tbsp sugar, 2 heaped and 1 level tbsp plain (all-purpose) flour, 40g/1½oz/3tbsp butter and 1 heaped and 1 level tbsp sugar for the crumble topping. Bake this for about 20 minutes.

serves 6

1kg/2lb/4 cups fruit – stewed apples or pears; rhubarb cut into chunks; plums, halved and stones (pits) removed; gooseberries, topped and tailed; bilberries, blueberries or blackcurrants, stems removed
3 rounded tbsp sugar

For the crumble
250g/9oz/1½ cups self-raising wholewheat flour or a half-and-half mix of white and wholewheat self-raising flour
175g/6oz/¾ cup butter
8 tbsp demerara sugar

Set the oven to 200°C/400°F/Gas 6. Put the fruit into a lightly greased large shallow ovenproof dish, add the sugar and mix gently; see that the fruit is in an even layer. Put the flour into a bowl and rub in the butter with your fingertips until the mixture looks like fine breadcrumbs and there are no obvious bits of butter showing. Add the sugar and mix gently. Spoon the crumble topping over the fruit in an even layer, covering all the fruit. Bake for 30–40 minutes, until the crumble is crisp and lightly browned and the fruit feels tender when pierced in the middle with a skewer.

treacle tart

You could replace some of the syrup with black treacle (molasses) if you prefer.

serves 4–6

First make the pastry: put the flour into a bowl with the salt and rub in the butter with your fingertips until the mixture looks like fine breadcrumbs. Press the mixture together to make a dough – as the proportion of butter is a little higher than usual, you shouldn't need to add any water. Set the oven to 200°C/400°F/Gas 6. Roll out the pastry and line a 20cm/8 inch tart pan or other suitable dish; trim the edges. Roll the trimmings into strips to make a lattice on top of the tart; set aside. Chill the pastry case and strips while you make the filling.

Put the golden syrup into a saucepan and heat gently to melt, then remove from the heat and add the crumbs and lemon juice. Spoon this mixture into the pastry case, level the surface, then arrange the strips in a lattice on top. Bake for 25 minutes, until the pastry is crisp and lightly browned. Serve warm.

For the pastry
125g/4oz/³/₄ cup + 2tbsp self-raising wholewheat flour or a half-and-half mix of white and wholewheat self-raising flour
½tsp salt
65g/2½oz/5tbsp butter

For the filling
6tbsp golden syrup
3 slices of wholewheat bread, made into crumbs
1tsp lemon juice

double-crust apple pie

A mixture of wholewheat and white flour gives this traditional pie a deliciously nutty flavour and a very appetizing appearance. Other fruits such as blackberries, or a mixture of blackberries and apples, rhubarb, pears, gooseberries or plums can be used: just cut or top and tail them as necessary and use them in place of the apples. If the fruit is very sharp, add more sugar, maybe up to 175g/6oz/scant 1 cup. To make a small pie, for one or two people, use a third of these quantities and bake for 15–20 minutes in a small dish.

serves 6

125g/4oz/¾ cup plain wholewheat flour
125g/4oz/¾ cup plain white (all-purpose) flour
125g/4oz/½ cup butter
3tbsp cold water
milk, to glaze

For the filling
750g/1½lb cooking (tart) apples, peeled, cored and sliced, plus 75g/3oz/ scant ½ cup sugar; or use 1 quantity of stewed fruit – see page 144 – prepared and cooled

Set the oven to 200°C/400°F/Gas 6. Sift the flours into a bowl, adding the bran left behind in the sieve (strainer) too. Rub in the butter until the mixture looks like bread-crumbs, then add the water to make a dough. Roll out just under half the pastry on a floured board and use to line a 20–23cm/8–9 inch shallow pie plate. Put the fruit on top, mixing it with the sugar if you're using uncooked fruit. Roll out the rest of the pastry and place on top of the fruit. Press the edges together firmly, trim the edges and crimp or press with the prongs (tines) of a fork. Make one or two steam holes. Brush with milk. Bake for about 30 minutes, until the pastry is crisp and lightly browned.

oven-baked egg custard

For each person, allow 1 egg, whisked and made up to 150ml/5fl oz/⅔ cup with milk, and 1 rounded tsp sugar. If you keep a jar of caster sugar with a vanilla pod (bean) in it, this will flavour the custard; otherwise add a drop or two of vanilla extract. Whisk all your ingredients together, pour the mixture into a suitable ovenproof container – a small ramekin for one person – stand the dish in a baking pan and pour hot water into the pan so that it reaches halfway up the dish. Bake in the oven at 180°C/350°F/ Gas 4 until the custard has set and a knife blade inserted in the middle comes out clean. This will take about 40–60 minutes. The custard can be served hot or chilled, which gives it a thicker, creamier texture. A little nutmeg grated over the top before baking is pleasant.

caramel custard

For each person put 1 rounded tbsp granulated sugar into a saucepan and heat until it melts and is golden brown. Remove from the heat, stand back and add 1tsp water for each serving. This will melt the caramel. Stir until smooth, then pour into an ovenproof dish, tipping the dish so that the caramel coats the base. Make the custard as described in the previous recipe and pour this on top of the caramel. Cook the custard as in the previous recipe. Cool and chill the custard, then loosen the edge by slipping the blade of a knife round inside the dish. Invert the dish over a serving plate and turn out the custard.

stove-top egg custard

Put 2 egg yolks into a bowl and blend to a smooth cream with 1 heaped tsp cornflour (cornstarch) and a little milk taken from 600ml/1 pint/ 2½ cups. Heat the rest of the milk to boiling point, then pour it over the cornflour (cornstarch) mixture, stir, and tip the whole mixture into the saucepan. Stir over the heat until the mixture thickens, then let it come to the boil. Boil for 30 seconds only, then remove from the heat immediately. Stir in 1 heaped tbsp vanilla sugar, or caster (superfine) sugar and a few drops of real vanilla extract. Serve hot or cold.

ice cream

You can use a batch of stove-top custard as a base for this, or use up leftover oven-baked custard. Just fold an equal quantity of whipping cream, lightly whipped, into the cold custard. Pour the mixture into a plastic container and freeze until the ice cream is getting firm round the edges, then give it a good whisking and put it back to finish freezing. Allow to stand at room temperature for 30 minutes before serving, then beat to make it smooth.

Another wonderful way of making ice cream is to mix 350ml/12fl oz/1½ cups sieved puréed fruit with 300ml/ 10fl oz/1¼ cups whipping cream and enough sugar to taste.

Or, for the simplest ice cream of all, whip together a 225g/8oz can condensed milk and 300ml/10fl oz/1¼ cups whipping cream. This is nice served with a sharp sauce made from puréed redcurrants or blackcurrants, slightly sweetened.

refrigerator cheesecake

This is a not-too-expensive special occasion dessert that's very easy to make. Quark is a very low fat soft white cheese. It makes up for the fat in the double (heavy) cream which is necessary to give the mixture body.

Mix together the crumbs and butter; press the mixture into the base of a 20cm/8 inch springform pan or other suitable shallow dish. Put the Quark, cream and sugar into a bowl and whisk together until thick; spoon the mixture on top of the crumb mixture and level off. Wash and halve the strawberries; arrange on top of the white cheese mixture. Pour the jelly over the top of the strawberries. Chill before serving.

refrigerator cheesecake for one

Crush 2 digestive biscuits (graham crackers) and mix with 1tbsp melted butter; press into a small ramekin or an individual-sized shallow tart pan. Beat together 50g/2oz/¼ cup Quark low fat soft white cheese and 2tbsp whipping cream, until the mixture holds its shape. Add 1 heaped tsp sugar. Spread the mixture on top of the crumbs. Arrange 50–125g/2–4oz strawberries on top, then spoon 1–2tbsp melted redcurrant jelly over the strawberries and leave to cool.

125g/4oz/1⅓ cups digestive biscuits (graham crackers), crushed
50g/2oz/¼ cup butter, melted
400g/14oz/1¾ cups Quark low fat soft white cheese
150ml/5fl oz/⅔ cup double (heavy) cream
3–4tbsp sugar

For the topping
225g/8oz strawberries
2–3tbsp redcurrant jelly, melted

baked cheesecake

In the winter this cheesecake is good topped with alternating circles of halved and deseeded purple and green grapes, and melted apricot jam, instead of the strawberries. For one or two people, make a half quantity – use a whole egg – in a 15cm/6 inch tart pan or dish; bake for 15–20 minutes.

serves 6

125g/4oz/1⅓ cups digestive biscuits (graham crackers), crushed
50g/2oz/¼ cup butter, melted
225g/8oz/1 cup curd or ricotta cheese
2tbsp sugar
1 egg, beaten
1tbsp lemon juice
a few drops of real vanilla extract

For the topping
225g/8oz strawberries
2–3tbsp redcurrant jelly, melted

Set the oven to 190°C/375°F/Gas 5. Mix together the crumbs and butter; press the mixture into the base of a 20cm/8 inch tart pan or other suitable shallow dish. Put the cheese and sugar into a bowl with the egg, lemon juice and vanilla and beat together until smooth. Pour the mixture on top of the crumb mixture. Bake for about 20 minutes until set in the middle. Turn off the oven and leave the cheesecake to cool in the oven: if it cools too quickly, it may crack.

To finish, wash and halve the strawberries and arrange on top of the cheesecake. Pour the jelly over the top of the strawberries. Chill before serving.

Making your own cakes not only saves money, but also enables you to know exactly what is going into them, and to use the best and healthiest ingredients. They needn't be time-consuming to make. Here are some very simple suggestions based on traditional methods, plus a recipe for a quick and easy bread thrown in for good measure.

express bakery

easy wholewheat scones

These can be whizzed up in no time and are delicious for a quick tea-time treat, especially with some jam and cream, or reduced sugar jam and thick yogurt if you're feeling virtuous.

makes 6–8

225g/8oz/1½ cups self-raising wholewheat flour or a half-and-half mix of white and wholewheat self-raising flour

2tsp baking powder

50g/2oz/¼ cup butter

1 egg, whisked and made up to 150ml/5fl oz/⅔ cup with 2tbsp milk

Set the oven to 220°C/425°F/Gas 7.

Sift the flour and baking powder into a bowl, adding the residue of bran from the sieve (strainer) as well, then add the butter and rub it in with your fingertips. Add the egg and milk mixture and mix to a soft but not sticky dough. Turn this out on to a floured board and knead lightly, then press out to a depth of at least 1cm/½ inch, so that the scones are nice and high when they're cooked. Cut the scones out with a 5cm/2 inch round cutter and place them on a floured baking sheet. Bake the scones for 12–15 minutes, until they're golden brown and the sides spring back when lightly pressed. Cool on a wire rack, or serve immediately.

cheese scones

These are delicious to eat warm from the oven, for a quick lunch or supper. They're good buttered, with a little salad, with some fresh firm tomatoes and crisp celery.

makes 6–8

Set the oven to 220°C/425°F/Gas 7.

Sift the flour, mustard powder and baking powder into a bowl, adding the residue of bran from the sieve (strainer) as well, then add the butter and rub it in with your fingertips. Add the egg and milk mixture and half the grated cheese and mix to a soft but not sticky dough. Turn this out on to a floured board and knead lightly, then press out to a depth of at least 1cm/½ inch, so that the scones are nice and high when they're cooked. Cut the scones out with a 5cm/2 inch round cutter and place them on a floured baking sheet. Sprinkle the rest of the grated cheese on top of the scones, then bake them for 12–15 minutes, until they're golden brown and the sides spring back when lightly pressed. Cool on a wire rack, or serve immediately.

225g/8oz/1½ cups self-raising wholewheat flour or a half-and-half mix of white and wholewheat self-raising flour
½tsp mustard powder
2tsp baking powder
25g/1oz/2tbsp butter
1 egg, whisked and made up to 150ml/5fl oz/⅔ cup with 2tbsp milk
75g/3oz/¾ cup grated cheese

wholewheat jam tarts

Children love this wholefood version of an old favourite. These tarts make useful lunch box treats for school.

makes 12

125g/4oz/¾ cup + 2tbsp plain wholewheat flour or a half-and-half mix of plain white (all-purpose) flour and wholewheat flour
50g/2oz/¼ cup butter
6tsp cold water

For the filling
4 heaped tbsp jam, preferably the reduced sugar type

Set the oven to 190°C/375°F/Gas 5.

Grease a shallow 12-hole bun tin (cup cake or muffin pan). Put the flour into a bowl; add the butter and rub it in with your fingertips until the mixture looks like breadcrumbs. Add the water, then press the mixture together to form a dough. Roll the pastry out carefully on a lightly floured board, then cut into 12 circles using a 6cm/2½ inch round cutter. Press a pastry circle lightly into each section of the tin (pan), then put 1 heaped tsp jam into each. Bake the jam tarts towards the top of the oven for about 10 minutes, until the pastry is lightly browned. Cool in the tin (pan).

date fingers

These crisp fingers rely on the dates for sweetness, with no added sugar.

makes 12–16

Set the oven to 200°C/400°F/Gas 6.

First prepare the filling: put the dates and water into a small saucepan and cook gently for 5–10 minutes until the dates are soft. Mash the dates, making sure that there are no hard pieces of stem or stone amongst them. Leave to cool.

To make the pastry, put the flour into a bowl with the salt and rub in the butter with your fingertips until the mixture looks like fine breadcrumbs. Add the water, then press the mixture together to make a dough. Divide the mixture in half. Roll out half to fit a Swiss (jelly) roll pan – or just roll it into an oblong roughly this size and place on a baking sheet if you prefer. Spread the date mixture on top of the pastry. Roll out the rest of the pastry to fit the top, press into position and trim the edges. Prick all over with a fork. Bake for 30 minutes, until the pastry is firm and lightly browned. Cool for 30 minutes in the pan, then cut into 12–16 fingers. Ease the fingers out of the pan and place on a wire rack to finish cooling.

225g/8oz/1½ cups self-raising wholewheat flour or a half-and-half mix of white and wholewheat self-raising flour
½tsp salt
125g/4oz/½ cup butter
3tbsp cold water

For the filling
225g/8oz/heaping 1½ cups dates – not sugar-rolled
150ml/5fl oz/⅔ cup water

quick and easy fruit cake

This cake made without eggs will keep for 7–10 days in an airtight tin.

**makes one 20cm/
8 inch round cake**

350g/12oz/2¼ cups plain
wholewheat flour or a
half-and-half mix of plain
white (all-purpose) flour
and wholewheat flour
1tsp ground mixed spice
175g/6oz/¾ cup butter
175g/6oz/scant 1 cup dark
brown sugar
225g/8oz/heaping 1½ cups
mixed dried fruit
grated rind of a
well-scrubbed orange
125g/4oz/¾ cup glacé
(candied) cherries, rinsed
and halved – optional
1 heaped tbsp ground
almonds – optional
125ml/4fl oz/½ cup milk
2tbsp vinegar
¾tsp bicarbonate of soda
(baking soda)

Set the oven to 150°C/300°F/Gas 2.

Grease a 20cm/8 inch round cake pan and line with a double layer of greased greaseproof (waxed) paper. Sift the flour and spice into a bowl, adding the residue of bran from the sieve (strainer) as well. Rub in the butter with your fingertips until the mixture resembles breadcrumbs, then add the dried fruit and orange rind, and the cherries and ground almonds if you're using these.

Warm half the milk in a small saucepan and add the vinegar. Dissolve the soda in the rest of the milk, then add to the milk and vinegar mixture. Quickly stir this into the flour and fruit, mixing well so that everything is combined. Spoon the mixture into the prepared cake pan. Bake for 2–2½ hours, until a skewer inserted into the middle of the cake comes out clean. Leave the cake in the pan to cool, then strip off the paper.

rock cakes

Easy to make, spicy and delicious eaten while still warm.

Set the oven to 200°C/400°F/Gas 6.

Sift the flour and spice into a bowl, adding the residue of bran from the sieve (strainer) as well, then rub in the butter with your fingertips until the mixture looks like fine breadcrumbs. Add two thirds of the sugar, the fruit and the egg and milk mixture. Mix lightly, so that the mixture just holds together. Put heaps of the mixture on to a greased baking sheet, leaving a little room around for spreading, then sprinkle with the rest of the sugar. Bake for about 15 minutes, until lightly browned. Leave to cool on a wire rack.

225g/8oz/1½ cups self-raising wholewheat flour or a half-and-half mix of white and wholewheat self-raising flour
½tsp ground mixed spice
125g/4oz/½ cup butter
3 rounded tbsp demerara sugar
125g/4oz/scant ¾ cup mixed dried fruit
1 egg, beaten with 1tbsp milk

flapjacks

One of the quickest recipes ever and popular with everyone.

makes 12–16

125g/4oz/½ cup butter

6 rounded tbsp dark brown sugar

1 slightly rounded tbsp golden syrup (or light corn syrup)

175g/6oz/2 cups rolled oats

Set the oven to 190°C/375°F/Gas 5.

Grease an 18 x 27.5cm/7 x 11 inch Swiss (jelly) roll pan. Put the butter, sugar and syrup into a large saucepan and heat gently until melted, then remove from the heat and stir in the oats. Mix well, then spread the mixture into the pan and press down evenly. Bake for 20 minutes, until brown all over. Mark into fingers while still hot, then leave in the pan until cold. The flapjacks become crisp as they cool, and keep well in an airtight tin.

gingerbread

This gingerbread gets sticky if you wrap it in foil and store it in an airtight tin for several days. It will keep well for 7–14 days.

makes 12 pieces

Set the oven to 170°C/325°F/Gas 3.

Grease a 20cm/8 inch square cake pan and line with greased greaseproof (waxed) paper. Melt the syrup, treacle (molasses), sugar and butter in a saucepan over a gentle heat. Cool.

Sift the flour, baking powder and ginger into a bowl, adding the residue of bran from the sieve (strainer) as well. Make a well in the middle and pour in the treacle mixture and the beaten eggs. Dissolve the soda in the milk, then stir this into the mixture. Pour the mixture into the prepared pan. Bake for 1½ hours, until well-risen and firm to touch. Cool in the pan, then turn out, strip off the paper and cut into slices.

1 heaped tbsp golden syrup
(or light corn syrup)
6 heaped tbsp black treacle
(molasses)
3 rounded tbsp dark
brown sugar
125g/4oz/½ cup butter
225g/8oz/1½ cups plain
wholewheat flour or a
half-and-half mix of plain
white (all-purpose) flour
and wholewheat flour
2tsp baking powder
½tsp ground ginger
2 eggs, beaten
½tsp bicarbonate of soda
(baking soda)
150ml/5fl oz/⅔ cup milk

all-in-one sponge cake

A lovely light cake that couldn't be easier to make.

125g/4oz/¾ cup + 2tbsp
self-raising wholewheat
flour or a half-and-half mix
of white and wholewheat
self-raising flour
1tsp baking powder
125g/4oz/heaping ½ cup
light brown sugar
125g/4oz/½ cup soft butter
2 eggs

For the filling and topping
3tbsp warmed jam,
preferably the reduced
sugar type
a little caster (superfine)
sugar

Set the oven to 170°C/325°F/Gas 3.

Grease two 18cm/7 inch sandwich (layer cake) pans with butter, then line the base of each with a circle of greased greaseproof (waxed) paper. Sift the flour and baking powder into a bowl, then add the sugar, butter and eggs. Beat with a wooden spoon or an electric mixer, until the mixture is smooth, thick and glossy. Spoon the mixture into the prepared pans, scraping round the edge of the bowl with a spatula. Level the top. Bake, without opening the oven door, for 30 minutes. Test whether the cakes are done by pressing them lightly in the middle with a fingertip: if the cake bounces back afterwards, it's done. Leave the cakes in the pans to cool for 1 minute, then turn them out on to a wire rack and carefully remove the paper. Leave the cakes to cool completely. Sandwich the cakes together with jam and sprinkle with sugar.

iced fingers

Made from the same mixture as in the recipe opposite, these are popular and easy to make.

makes 12–16 slices

Set the oven to 170°C/325°F/Gas 3.

Grease and line an 18 x 27.5cm/7 x 11 inch shallow cake pan. Sift the flour and baking powder into a bowl, then add the sugar, butter and eggs. Beat with a wooden spoon or an electric mixer, until the mixture is smooth, thick and glossy. Spoon the mixture into the prepared pan, scraping round the edge of the bowl with a spatula. Level the top. Bake, without opening the oven door, for 30 minutes. Test whether the cake is done by pressing it lightly in the middle with a fingertip: if the cake bounces back afterwards, it's done. Leave to cool in the pan while you make the icing.

Put the icing (confectioners') sugar into a bowl and beat in the water a little at a time until you have a thick mixture. Spread the icing over the top of the sponge, then lift the whole thing out of the pan, using the paper to pick it up, and place on a wire rack. Cut into sections when cold. You can decorate each piece with chopped nuts, sugar strands (sprinkles or vermicelli) or a piece of glacé (candied) cherry, if liked.

125g/4oz/¾ cup + 2tbsp self-raising wholewheat flour or a half-and-half mix of white and wholewheat self-raising flour
1tsp baking powder
125g/4oz/heaping ½ cup light brown sugar
125g/4oz/½ cup soft butter
2 eggs

For the icing
4 heaped tbsp icing (confectioners') sugar
1–2tbsp water

quick buns

makes 12

175g/6oz/1¼ cups
self-raising wholewheat
flour or a half-and-half mix
of white and wholewheat
self-raising flour
125g/4oz/½ cup soft butter
4 rounded tbsp sugar
2 eggs

For the icing and topping
4 heaped tbsp icing
(confectioners') sugar
1–2tbsp water
chopped nuts, or a few
chocolate sugar strands
(sprinkles or vermicelli) or
sliced glacé (candied)
cherries

Set the oven to 190°C/375°F/Gas 5.

Thoroughly grease a shallow 12-hole bun tin (cup cake or muffin pan). Sift the flour into a bowl, adding any bran from the sieve (strainer) as well, then put in the butter, sugar and eggs and beat well with a wooden spoon or an electric mixer, until all the ingredients are well-blended and the mixture is thick and slightly glossy looking. Drop a good heaped teaspoonful of the mixture into each section of the tin (pan). Bake for 15–20 minutes until the cakes have risen and feel firm to a light touch. Let the cakes cool for a couple of minutes, then ease them out with a knife and leave them to cool on a wire rack.

To make the icing, put the icing (confectioners') sugar into a bowl and beat in the water a little at a time until you have a thick mixture. Spread a little icing on top of each cake and decorate with your chosen topping.

easy shortbread

Set the oven to 150°C/300°F/Gas 2.

Put the butter and sugar into a bowl and cream together until the sugar is blended, then add the flour and mix together to form a dough. Put the dough on to a floured surface, kneading it slightly, then press it into a 20cm/8 inch tart pan. Prick the top and bake for 1¼–1½ hours until set and just beginning to go golden. Mark into sections with a knife, then leave to cool in the pan.

To make shortbread biscuits, roll the mixture out about 3mm/⅛ inch thick, cut into circles and place on a baking sheet. Bake for about 30 minutes.

175g/6oz/¾ cup butter
75g/3oz/scant ½ cup soft brown sugar
250g/9oz/heaping1½ cups plain wholewheat flour or a half-and-half mix of plain white (all-purpose) flour and wholewheat flour

wholewheat bread

This is a very quick bread to make as it doesn't have any kneading.

makes two
450g/1lb loaves

450g/1lb/heaping 3 cups plain wholewheat flour

2tsp salt

1 sachet (package) easy-blend (rapid-rise) dried yeast

1tbsp honey, molasses or black treacle

about 350ml/12fl oz/ 1½ cups tepid water

Grease two 450g/1lb loaf pans (each measuring about 18 x 10 x 7.5cm/6 x 4 x 3 inches) thoroughly with butter. Put the flour, salt and yeast into a large bowl. Mix together the honey, molasses or treacle and the water; stir well, then add this to the flour. Mix well to make a dough that is just too soft to knead. Divide the dough in half and place one half in each pan. Cover loosely with cling film (plastic wrap) and leave in a warm place – or on the kitchen work surface – until the dough has risen by one third. This will take 30–45 minutes, depending on the temperature of the room.

Fifteen minutes or so before the bread is ready, set the oven to 230°C/450°F/Gas 8.

Bake the loaves for 35 minutes. Turn the loaves out of their pans and put them on a wire rack to cool.

index